LUXURIOUS

INTERIORS

BREATHTAKING HOMES BY AMERICA'S FINEST INTERIOR DESIGNERS

Published by

PANACHE
P A N A C H E   P A R T N E R S

Panache Partners, LLC
Dallas, Texas
469.246.6060
Fax: 469.246.6062
www.panache.com

Publishers: Brian G. Carabet and John A. Shand

Printed in Malaysia

Distributed by Independent Publishers Group
800.888.4741

PUBLISHER'S DATA

Luxurious Interiors

Library of Congress Control Number: 2014900072

ISBN 13: 978-0-9886140-4-8
ISBN 10: 0988614049

First Printing 2014

10 9 8 7 6 5 4 3 2 1

Right: Orlando Diaz-Azcuy Design Associates, page 539

Previous Page: Pepe Calderin Design, page 351

Panache Partners, LLC, is dedicated to the restoration and conservation
of the environment. Our books are manufactured with strict adherence
to an environmental management system in accordance with ISO 14001
standards, including the use of paper from mills certified to derive their
products from well-managed forests. We are committed to continued
investigation of alternative paper products and environmentally responsible
manufacturing processes to ensure the preservation of our fragile planet.

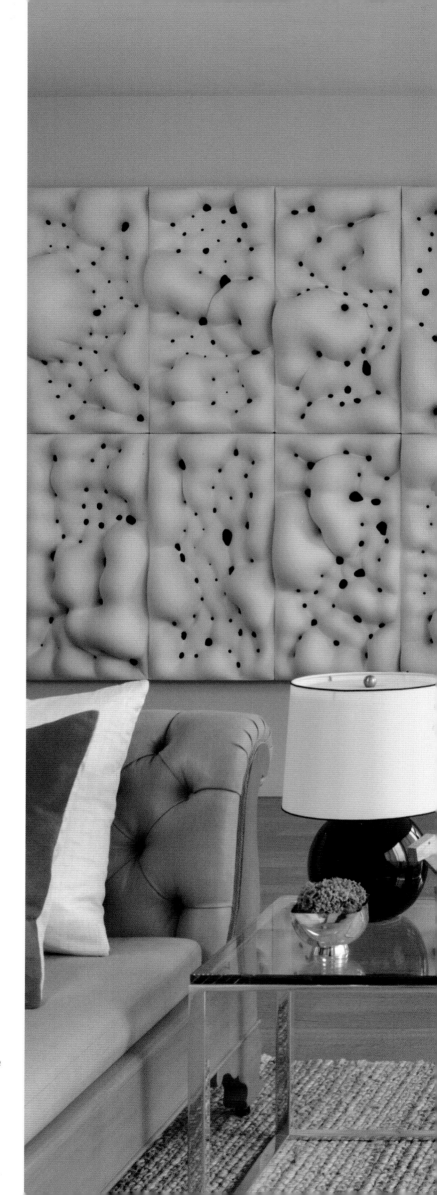

LUXURIOUS INTERIORS

introduction

JMA Interior Decoration, page 269

Simultaneously exhilarating and formidable, the process of interior design is unlike any other undertaking. To extract the essence that will reflect those living within the home, designers must embark on a journey through the homeowner's life. The process requires knowledge of multiple disciplines, energy and enthusiasm to persevere over time, and a keen ability to understand and communicate with a plethora of personalities.

Interior designers must also take into account the contrasting principles at work in each home: each room needs to have its own flavor yet flow with the rest of the home; the design should be relevant to modern life and still be timeless in aesthetic; and the living space must function as a private sanctuary as well as a haven for entertaining visitors.

Luxurious Interiors boasts the impressive work of professionals who effortlessly meet all of the challenges of design, expressing the homeowner's lifestyle and sense of style in ways never even dreamed. This book lays the foundation for inspiration through unparalleled images that present an insider's look into private retreats, and delves even deeper as the experts reveal their philosophies and advice gleaned through years of experience.

Within this extraordinary collection, you'll find high-rise condos transformed from stark to stunning, suburban estates with inspiring views, and weekend cottages that beckon relaxation from everyday life. From the coast to the lake, from the mountains to the cities, these designers passionately redefine what it means to turn a house into a home.

Sagart Studio, page 107

Studio Santalla, page 167

Northeast

Michael Shannon Designs, page 147

"Your home is your sanctuary. Fill it with things that support, nurture, and inspire you." Ginger Atherton

Matthew Yee, Inc., page 143

Lori Shinal Interiors, page 91

Haleh Design, page 25

The Patterson Group, page 99

northeast

Dmitry Dudnik

New York

Before launching his own interior design firm in 2005, Dmitry Dudnik studied design, painting, and decorative arts at the Stieglitz Academy of Art and Design in St. Petersburg, Russia, where he was born. His aesthetic was influenced by the city's majestic palaces and mansions, which he helped restore as a student through the city's various historical restoration projects. He arrived in New York in 1990 and contributed to decorative projects with companies like Slatkin & Co., Thomas Britt, Inc., and Mario Buatta. Dmitry also participated in the Kips Bay Decorator Show House and in the Hampton Designer Showhouse. His elegant interiors possess a refined quality and his spaces are graceful and inviting, integrating his knowledge of art history with a love for classical design. Today his keen attention to detail and nuanced sense of color, proportion, and texture provide the foundation for the home designs of his international clientele.

Left: The grand living room, unfinished when the project was acquired, evokes the illusion of a bygone era. The room's impressive height is softened by luxurious silk drapery in crimson and gold. A blend of antique objects and paintings, custom antique reproductions, and ornate decorative details creates an authentic period feel.
Photographs by Anthony Trofymoff

"Fine interiors should possess the dimension of a wonderfully executed work of art." *Dmitry Dudnik*

Above Left & Facing Page: An early 19th-century Italian painting rests above delicate fine china. The painting's elaborate frame complements the gilded French figurines below. Plush fabrics and elaborate trimmings give the room warmth.

Above Right: A variety of stones and handpainted Spanish tile work combine in a lavish shower room that's fit for royalty.
Photographs by Anthony Trofymoff

Above & Facing Page: In the orangerie, an onyx and marble inlaid floor provides interest without overshadowing the spectacular view through the glass ceiling. An Italian table with ornamental engravings on the glass top is balanced by an early 20th-century gilded bronze chandelier.

Right: An early 20th-century majolica planter and Sevres vases are in keeping with the home's predilection for pieces that are highly crafted and colorfully detailed.
Photographs by Anthony Trofymoff

Essence of Design

Maryland

Shiva Rostami founded Essence of Design in 2005, combining her love of travel and other cultures, and architecture with an impressive repertoire of interior design experience and education. Shiva particularly enjoys working with fabrics, and will often take a fabric and design the room around that. Instead of simple window panels, in many cases she will take great joy in adding swags and cornices, cartouches with elaborate trim and moulding. It's all part of her extremely hands-on design style; she loves staying involved in every detail. A seasoned traveler, Shiva frequently imbues her rooms with her favorite European-style décor and architectural touches. Respected publications like *Luxury Homes Quarterly* and *Home & Design Portfolio* have also recognized Shiva, the latter naming her one of 100 Top Designers.

Left: Black stone tops the end tables, which flank the sofa and balance out the Baroque coffee table done in a black and gold finish. Richly detailed window treatments grace the floor-to-ceiling windows.
Photographs by Bob Narod

"The details are essential to a design's success."
Shiva Rostami

Top: Two double-sided arched entryways and a curved wrought-iron staircase make a grand statement from the vantage point of the living room. The owners hold many functions in the home, both political and personal, so an open floor plan was of utmost importance. A row of three Italian frescoes with marble tile frames is in keeping with the colors and European style the owners love.

Bottom: The powder room features an Italian Bombay chest that we turned into a stunning, functional vanity. A richly carved gold mirror takes center stage, flanked by crystal sconces. Adding another touch of luxury, a gorgeous Schonbek chandelier hangs in front of red and gold wallpaper. Even the floor is detailed with glamour—black galaxy tiles accented with gold inserts.

Facing Page Top: It took more than a year to gain the homeowners' confidence to use a deep rose and gold palette in the dining room, which resulted in a warm and cozy ambience. The ceiling detailing echoes the colors from the piano room, while two semi-flush crystal chandeliers allow the table to be moved for catered parties. Touches of blue in the artwork above the fireplace, in the table runner, and in the window treatments match colors from the adjacent rooms.

Facing Page Bottom: A dramatic aubergine palette characterizes the master suite. The sitting room at one end contains an heirloom fireplace as a magnificent focal point. The plush chenille chairs take advantage of the cozy fire and the flatscreen TV housed in the entertainment unit-wet bar across the room. Alcove lighting finishes out the romantic mood. Custom-made swags fill in the large spaces between the crown moulding and the palladium windows.
Photographs by Bob Narod

Above: The grand home's piano room contains minimal furniture for an open and airy feel. Simple but elegant window treatments in deep rose and gold tie into the colors of the adjacent dining room.

Left: In the living room, an eye-catching animal-print Versace rug inspired the color scheme and brings a magnificent detailing to the floor; the well-balanced colors exert an energy that is at once calm and inviting.

Facing Page: The master bedroom suite called for a custom-made sofa to perfectly fit the space and the style. Patterned fabrics were limited to the embroidered silk on the swags and jabots on the window treatment, and the custom ottomans at the foot of the bed. Despite the interplay of contrasting textures—silk, chenille, metallic linen, sateen, velvet—a subtle rhythm envelops the space. The shimmering beaded wallpaper acts as a gorgeous backdrop to showcase a painting by Ovissi, a personal gift from the artist.

Photographs by Bob Narod

Haleh Design

Maryland

The daughter of a textile innovator, Haleh Alemzadeh Niroo's life has been shaped by an early embrace of and consistent devotion to the design discipline. She gained cultural immersion and passion for classical design through a traditional education in Switzerland and France. Exposure to such 17th- and 18th-century architectural masterpieces as Versailles molded her instinct for proportion and appreciation for detailed workmanship. Formal design study and firsthand construction knowledge further inform her experience. For two decades as an architectural designer, Haleh has created timeless homes, often collaborating with husband and builder David Niroo, of Niroo Masterpieces. Her designs demonstrate her intuition for proportion, refined lavishness, and an eye for Old World detailing. Haleh travels the world sourcing distinctive pieces, and partners with elite companies such as Armando Rho, Colombo Mobili, Meroni, Rubli, Habersham, Highland Court, Lalique, and Herend to offer her clientele custom-made furnishings, fabrics, and one-of-a-kind accessories that are exceptional, singular, and distinctive.

Left: Working with the sweeping space of the foyer required me to call on my keen awareness of scale and proportion. The 20-foot-wide dome rising 32 feet above the marble floor demanded massive projections to effectively communicate the lush detail of the ceiling treatment, frieze, mouldings, and the magnitude of the 10-foot-wide Schonbek chandelier. Periods meld in the Corinthian columns and the transitional stair railing gilded in gold; a contemporary bronze statue by Gaylord Ho sits adjacent to an 18th-century mirror. The wall insets on the landing and second level are Fromental silk and hand-embroidered. The Colombo Mobili console at right boasts a rare Porto Gold marble top, complemented by a Lalique Angelique jar and Foo "good luck" dogs, limited-edition from Herend. The Persian rug is Qom silk; the Chene table is Lalique.
Photograph by Gordon Beall

"Refined luxury
expressed through
beautifully executed
detail is a central tenet
of my approach."
Haleh Alemzadeh Niroo

Above: In the grand salon, I addressed the space by keying in to the architecture and accentuating such features as the Corinthian columns, the ceiling treatment, crown moulding, and goldleaf detail. A subdued color palette and elegant yet intimate arrangement of furnishings allow these dramatic elements to claim center stage, while quietly reinforcing the inherent beauty of the room.

Facing Page: Paintings by French artists Emile-Auguste Hublin and Adolphe Bouguereau from the owner's 19th-century collection embody quiet luxury. Layered textures in velvet and silk are found throughout in such details as the window treatments, the cornice trim, and the passementerie on the sheers. The limited-edition vase is Lalique.
Photographs by Gordon Beall

Above Left & Right: The ceiling fresco depicting an Old World map imparts a warm patina reinforced throughout the library by such elements as the Italian chandelier in alabaster and antique brass and built-in inlaid Italian cabinetry from Armando Rho. Tradition melds with the new in the Marsan table and the limited edition Passeraux vase, both from Lalique. Cut velvet damask and solid velvet cornices pair with linen sheers to create layered textures.

Facing Page Top: In the tea room, a plaster wall treatment is faux-finished in goldleaf to accentuate detail. On display are the owners' collection of antique and limited-edition Herend tea sets. An elegant Waterford crystal chandelier crowns the design.

Facing Page Bottom: The dining room features a full-on embrace of pink orchestrated in a multitude of notes from a frothy milky tone to raspberry, salmon, and coral. The dramatic and layered window treatment includes Austrian sheers with damask panels and center swags. The pattern of the cornice and swag repeats in the chair backs. The plaster wall treatment accented in goldleaf emphasizes the dramatic projections of the mouldings, which echo in the gilded table base. The candelabra is Saint Louis, the place settings are custom-made by Herend, and the furnishings are from Colombo Mobili. The painting by Vittorio Reggianni is called "Eavesdropping."
Photographs by Gordon Beall

"Supreme elegance begins with comfort, the most important element of all."
Haleh Alemzadeh Niroo

Above & Right: The barrel-ceilinged master bedroom called for serene coloration; blue brought an intimacy to the scale of the room. The walls were faux-finished in an elegant silk stripe; a Lombardy 19th-century bed and comfortable Colombo Mobili furniture in European plum walnut with cherry inlay add warmth. Lalique Josephine lamps complete the room. A Max Carlier painting hangs near the ornate-framed mirror, with a Francis Hayman painting parallel to it on the other side.

Facing Page Top: In a kitchen that exudes Old World style, the faux-finished walls accent the tonalities of the custom Habersham cabinetry. The window treatment allows for natural sunlight to shine in and dresses the wall in a Highland Court floral silk. Venetian gold granite countertops round out the sophisticated space.

Facing Page Bottom Left: The owner's passion for glass artist Lalique is displayed though a number of limited-edition pieces, such as a perfume bottle and turtle dove lamp. Taking center stage, a plum walnut dresser by Colombo Mobili is inlaid with zebrawood and yew.

Facing Page Bottom Right: The tub faced in dark emperador honed mosaic sits centered in the master bath to accentuate the double-vaulted ceiling. A metallic finish imparts an Old World feel to the Habersham vanity. Murals painted in the three lunettes depict landscape and water elements. The Schonbek chandelier and sconces and Habersham chaise complete the space.
Photographs by Gordon Beall

Kotzen Interiors

Massachusetts

From casually elegant to chic traditional, the spaces designed by Barbara Kotzen are as individual as the homeowners who live in them. For Barbara, principal designer of Kotzen Interiors, how a room feels is paramount. Warmth, depth, and attention to detail characterize her spaces and she believes that custom designs and architectural features go hand-in-hand. From hand-scraped millwork to plush pillows, each detail in Barbara's spaces is selected with attention to the feelings these elements will evoke in the owners. Her designs are practical, with a balance between light and dark, hard and soft. Her excitement is catching and her dedication to a project is unending. This is what brings homeowners back to her time and again for their primary and vacation residences.

Left: The Wolf Creek Ranch home sits on one of the 160-acre estates in the 14,000-acre development outside of Heber City, Utah. Outdoor patio areas capitalize on the sweeping views of the Wasatch Mountains to the west and the Uinta Mountains to the north and northeast. Custom-designed furniture offers the homeowners a comfortable place to gather and dine while admiring the views. Branch-like railing merges seamlessly with the surrounding landscape.
Photograph courtesy of Richard Mandelkorn

"Good design is a
beautiful yet practical
interpretation of vision."
Barbara Kotzen

Top: Although the front of the home is understated and nestled among the trees, the back of the home cascades down the mountain and features windows in nearly every room. The first floor and basement open to the back of the property. Through the back gate of the lot, the homeowners have direct access to the Uinta National Forest, over two million acres of preserved forest.

Facing Page: All of the ceilings, floors, and exterior eaves of the house were constructed of reclaimed wood. Deadfall trees were used for timbers whenever possible for the geothermal home. The kitchen features elegant stonework, built-in appliances, and a custom copper hood. The rustic stairway leads to the only second-story space in the house, a loft that overlooks the great room.
Photographs courtesy of Richard Mandelkorn

Above: In the great room, a two-story natural wood fireplace serves as the focal point. Guests have multiple seating options under the majestic chandelier and lofty beamed ceilings. The light colored walls accentuate the rough-hewn details of the wood and the rug grounds the space, adding depth and warmth.

Facing Page Top: The cozy dining room features simple and elegant furnishings, rustic light fixtures, and a design plan that emphasizes views of the 150-year-old Aspens.

Facing Page Bottom: The kitchen looks into a cozy gathering room. Lower ceilings and comfortable seating invite quiet conversation or reading. A smaller dining table behind the sofa is perfect for family dinners.
Photographs courtesy of Richard Mandelkorn

Above: The master bathroom is the epitome of luxury. Copper sinks, hidden storage, and limestone mosaic tile give the room a rustic elegance consistent with the rest of the home. The large bathtub is surrounded by wincows to capitalize on the view.

Right: A corner fireplace, high beamed ceilings, and a subtle wall color create a quiet retreat for the homeowners. The console under the window contains a television that may be raised when in use, otherwise leaving the view uninterrupted.

Facing Page: Tones of blue and brown distinguish the homeowner's office, which provides a place for working, reading, or relaxing by the fire.
Photographs courtesy of Richard Mandelkorn

Above: The reclaimed wood ceiling and upholstered walls make the media room a warm retreat for family and friends. One of the few spaces in the home without views to the outdoors, the room is designed with two tiers—one with sectional seating and the other with theater seating.

Facing Page Top & Bottom Left: Each of the 10 guest rooms is different. The various color schemes reflect the rustic nature of the landscape surrounding the home. Wooden beds and furniture blend seamlessly with the rooms' reclaimed beams and hand-scraped millwork. Custom-made doors lead to a balcony or patio from each bedroom.

Facing Page Bottom Right: Each bunk room features built-in storage and trundles that pull out to sleep more guests. When the trundles are used, up to 10 people can sleep in each bunk room.
Photographs courtesy of Richard Mandelkorn

"Throughout the design process I carefully consider every detail—from texture and scale to color and lighting—to create an atmosphere that truly becomes an extension of my client's personality."
Barbara Kotzen

Pat Bibbee Designs

West Virginia

For award-winning designer Pat Bibbee, interior design isn't just about multiple concept boards and final installations; it's about ongoing conversations and lasting relationships. Pat Bibbee Designs, the design firm she established in Charleston in 1982, has garnered rave reviews both regionally and nationally from homeowners who count on Pat's experienced eye, personal approach, and fresh, creative thinking to transform simple rooms into works of art. Whether advising a first-time homeowner on furniture arrangement and color choices or revitalizing an entire home or vacation retreat, Pat Bibbee's signature style isn't a look, but a feel—a beautifully designed house that actually feels like home. Pat brings that same passion for blending atmosphere and style to her work for country clubs, offices, and high-profile cultural and civic landmarks, including Charleston's renowned Clay Center for the Arts and the West Virginia Governor's Mansion.

Left: For the couple's dining room, I focused on reflecting casual, reserved elegance. Rather than hanging paintings on every wall, I used sculptures to add dimension: The floating magnolia plates resemble a work of art. Repeated aqua and neutral tones throughout the home allow one room to flow into the next.
Photographs by Gwen Hunt

Above: Mixing textures and patterns is a trademark of what I do best. The stripes, plaids, and florals combine to create a serene and luxurious master bedroom.

Facing Page Top: The comfortable living room offers a sweeping view of the peppered pines outside, drawing the sage and sky-blue hues out of the room and creating a relaxing space that seems to flow out into nature.

Facing Page Bottom: In the small dining area, mint, seafoam, evergreen, and sage join to evoke a soft, welcoming ambience. Dark wood and a custom chandelier add elegance and warmth to the room, while an oversized bench invites guests to relax while dining.
Photographs by Gwen Hunt

Above & Facing Page: A mountain home that reflects the personality and interests of the homeowners, it's a gathering place for a larger family that can withstand lots of activity, pets, and guests. Fabrics and furnishings are a mix of old and new, a true reflection of the homeowners' hobbies and family history.
Photographs by Gwen Hunt

"Homes should be inviting. There aren't any velvet ropes in homes anymore." *Pat Bibbee*

Top: The Navajo-inspired rug sets the tone in the room for comfortable, relaxed living. The mixture of texture and pattern complement the large-scale pattern of the rug.

Middle: I wanted the guest bedroom to be a quiet retreat, reflecting the outdoors in a sophisticated blend of texture and color.

Bottom: The highly textured Stark carpeting, warm neutral tones, and luxurious velvets of the study offer an intimate spot for conversation. The tree-inspired drapery fabric is a nod to the wooded setting.

Facing Page: A custom rug by New River Artisans anchors the large dining table and chairs. The neutral backdrop sets off a large oil portrait of the homeowner, painted by my daughter, Alison Bibbee.
Photographs by Gwen Hunt

Amanda Maier Design

Pennsylvania

World travel and exposure to a variety of cultures inform the designs of Amanda Maier, who believes that interiors directly affect a homeowner's state of mind. After a successful career as a fashion model, Amanda turned her attention to pursuing another creative profession. Always interested in design—as a child she asked her mother for subscriptions to *Architectural Digest*— Amanda graduated with her bachelor's in interior design from the Art Institute of Philadelphia, apprenticed with various prestigious designers, and in 2007 branched out on her own to found Amanda Maier Design. Spaces created by Amanda integrate a beautiful combination of the natural world with a bit of Old Hollywood glamour. The balance between functionality and style is paramount to the designer, who loves to bring her special kind of energy and excitement to a home.

Left: I love texture: A burlap lampshade, warm wood tones, and bronze accents create both tactile and visual texture. The turned legs of the high console table play against the clean lines created by the doorway and coffee table. Gauzy draperies that softly filter sunlight make the room a warm, cozy space for entertaining and everyday life.
Photograph by Damon Landry

"Knowing when to edit a design is key. Negative space enhances what you bring to the room."
Amanda Maier

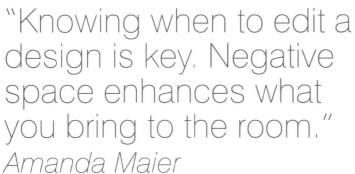

Above Left: The homeowners wanted to add a wow factor to the casual tone of their dining room. In the award-winning space, I used metallic accents to create a unique luminescence. From the four different metallic colors on the ceiling to the custom pressed-glass tabletop with twigs embedded in the glass, the room embraces both the luxurious and the natural. Basketweave grasscloth adorns the ceiling under its shimmery finish. The chandelier's organic shape and walnut hardwoods join traditional pieces in the form of a chinoiserie chest on gold leafed base, flanked by gold convex mirrors.

Above Right: I kept the beautiful front door when I moved it outward in the foyer addition. Adding the stained glass panels around the door not only emphasizes the existing glass in the piece itself, but also creates a Spanish-inspired entry to the home that reminds me of Antoni Gaudi's modernist architecture.

Facing Page Top Left: The master bathroom wasn't huge, so I maximized the square footage by placing the shower in the corner, extending the limestone walls to the ceiling and far wall, and building the tub deck into an extension of the shower to create a seat. Oil-rubbed bronze fixtures and the mosaic tile create an impression that Old World meets the new in the space.

Facing Page Top Right: Reclaimed Brazilian rosewood was used to create the custom vanity in the bathroom. The train-style overhead lamp and the rotated quatrefoil mirror create vintage interest in a modern construction.

Facing Page Bottom: French plaster walls give the master bedroom a beautiful glow and depth. The room was a bit awkward and blocky before we created a barrel ceiling and niche, which suggests a Tuscan feel. A black-and-white Charlie Waite photograph, custom mahogany sapele wood valances, and puddled draperies create a romantic atmosphere. Mismatched hardwoods add to the environment, giving the room a custom element.
Photographs by Damon Landry

Calder Design Group

New York

Fashion is often a portal through which designers discover their passion for interiors, and for Nicholas Calder it was no different. A career that began in fashion illustrating evolved into crafting visual displays before transitioning into interior design, the path Nicholas has been following since the 1970s. The ability to grasp and work in practically any style has made Calder Design Group a favorite for homeowners seeking to put their own unique stamp on their residences. Through deep understanding, communication, and collaboration, Nicholas, his daughter Melanie, and their team create rooms that reflect not only what the inhabitants admire and enjoy, but also what works best for their lifestyles.

Left: The modern, linear staircase juxtaposes beautifully against the organic texture of the tree trunk chairs and gently rounded table. Architectural simplicity at its most pure, the snowy white color accentuates the yin and yang of the entryway's design.
Photograph by Peter Rymwid Architectural Photography

Above & Facing Page Top: Bursts of lime, terra cotta, and lemon yellow lend a tropical feel to the lounge area, while textural elements and plenty of natural light distance the living area from the "white box" feel so common in New York City apartments.

Left: Designed for when the homeowners wish to dine intimately, the cozy nook with its built-in banquette is also the perfect place to seat children during large dinner celebrations.

Facing Page Bottom: A family den evokes the easygoing aura of the seashore with its earthy furnishings and relaxed floorplan. The cylindrical light fixtures provide ample illumination for reading while echoing the lines in the white planked walls and ceiling.
Photographs by Peter Rymwid Architectural Photography

Candice Adler Design

New Jersey

Candice Adler has always loved design, so when it came time to find an outlet for her creativity she turned her passion into a career in interiors. After gaining exposure for her work refurbishing vintage pieces, she became a buyer for a large furniture store where she purchased items suitable for all styles and tastes. The experience served as the foundation for her design flexibility; her approach encompasses all styles and tones to the specifications of homeowners. According to Candice, her job is an incredible responsibility that includes making a room beautiful, functional, and when necessary, family friendly. A space is only as good as it makes homeowners feel, and Candice's down-to-earth attitude and attention to detail ensure that homes make their owners feel special.

Left: Ornate wallpaper in a soft shade complements the delicate chandelier in the master bedroom. I combined a variety of patterns in the same color scheme to create a visually interesting yet tranquil space for the homeowners to relax in. The strong silhouette of the headboard against the damask pattern wallpaper gives the room Old World drama, while the corner mirror and streamlined draperies lend a contemporary flair to the design.
Photograph by E Z Memories

"More than anything else, lighting elevates the status of a space." *Candice Adler*

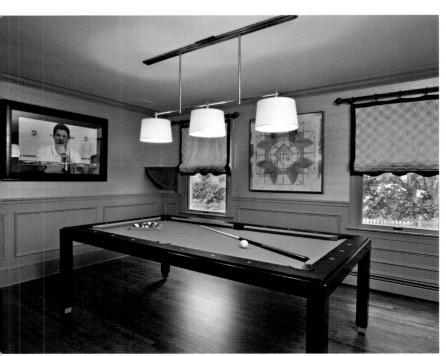

Top: The den's custom built-in unit, with its handpainted finish, gives the room much needed storage. A warm paint tone at the back of the shelves gives the piece depth. Swivel chairs offer a pop of pattern to the den and create a comfortable conversation space around the narrow six-legged cocktail table.
Photograph by E Z Memories

Middle & Bottom: The multifunctional space was a huge challenge: The husband wanted a game room and the wife wanted a formal dining room. To accomplish this, I placed a dining table in the middle of the space. For formal events, chairs in a mix of leather and fabric with nailhead trim serve as comfortable seating and encourage guest to linger at the table. When it's time for a guys' night in, the table rises to the appropriate height on hydraulic lifts and the wenge wood tabletop is removed to reveal a pool table underneath. The room's mirror transforms into a television. Grasscloth wallpaper and painted wainscoting work well for both functions, giving the room a sophisticated feel.
Photographs by E Z Memories

Facing Page Top: For a beach house, I brought elements of the ocean inside to create a soothing space for the homeowners to get away. The large pattern of the coffered ceiling draws the eye upward to the custom chandelier adorned with seaglass crystals. Soft linen drapery panels lend the room a casual and airy feel while the reclaimed wood dining table offers the space texture and character. I love the uncomplicated color scheme; it's so peaceful.
Photograph by Studio 53

Facing Page Bottom: Barstools that coordinate with the dining chairs create the perfect beach style for a seaside vacation home. The open flow of the grand room allows for easy movement throughout the space. Contrasting paint on the ceiling and millwork and the stone tile work on the fireplace wall create a palette inspired by the outdoor scenery. Built-in cabinets provide ample storage for books, games, and decorative accessories.
Photograph by Studio 53

Above: Sexy lines and the low-profile silhouette of the top-stitched leather sofas make the pieces a bold focal point of the great room. The outline of wood on the armchairs means they look great from any angle. An adjacent breakfast area in warm tones and an open chandelier make for an intimate space to share a meal.
Photograph by Studio 53

Right: A sitting area in the master bedroom is subtle and elegant. Small details like the quilted fabric on the backs of the chairs make the area a stunning entrance into the suite. Contrasting pillows on the sofa coordinate with the window treatments behind the piece, and the elements of the room stand out against the background of the tranquil hue on the walls.
Photograph by Studio 53

Facing Page Top: Handhoned recycled beams create a rustic feel in the great room. Rugged texture on the windows contrasts against the luxurious trims and fabric details in the room while jewel tones give it a rich ambience.
Photograph by E Z Memories

Facing Page Bottom: A green marble fireplace was transformed using specialty rusting paints and finishes to create its custom distressed quality. Varied patterns, intricate fabrics and trims, and the homeowners' unique collections make the space one of a kind. A glittering chandelier draws the eye to the piano. White crown moulding and tall white baseboards unify the space.
Photograph by E Z Memories

Fuller Interiors

Pennsylvania

Flipping through the pages of *Seventeen* magazine as a teenager, Jennifer Fuller became inspired by the dream bedrooms featured in the monthly publication. After an apprenticeship with Greensboro, North Carolina, designer Lindsay Henderson, Jennifer founded Fuller Interiors in 1999. Since then, she's never taken a day off from design—even when on vacation, she captures photographs of hotel lobbies, suites, and vintage buildings as inspiration. Merging classic style with a contemporary edge, Jennifer's designs are part Old Hollywood, part au courant luxury, all with an edge. Imbuing homes with a sense of soul that reflects the owners, she brings modern sensibility and contemporary elegance to timeless design. Jennifer believes in thinking outside the box, embracing bold colors, and knowing all the rules of conventional design so that she can break them.

Left: In a side nook off the kitchen, I created a space I like to call the summer room. Although it is a long, thin area, built-in bookcases and oversized chaises make the cozy space functional and welcoming. An authentic zebra hide rug stretches atop the ebony floors. I wanted the space to remain true to the architecture, but touches like the hot pink pillows that remind me of Chanel tweed suits, the vintage light fixture, and the contrasting black and white patterns create an edginess that speaks to modern design.
Photograph by Julia Lehman-McTigue

"Great design is all about the willingness to take risks." *Jennifer Fuller*

Top: Neutral color palettes with a pop of a vibrant color make the most impact. When paired with the black accents on the walls and in the furnishings, the bright orange chair is a great conversation piece. Completing the look, a lacquered Greek key coffee table, a seagrass rug, and an oversized mirror make a bold statement.

Middle: A small den off the living room provides a cozy space for the homeowners to hibernate. The room, which boasts custom bookshelves that feature a collection of objects, a curvy vintage sculpture, mirrored cabinets over the built-in bar, and warm earth tones, is crowned by the ceiling, which I covered in shimmery wallpaper that reflects light from the drum fixture hung just inches below.

Bottom: The homeowners wanted their living room to embody luxury. High-gloss orange paint on the ceiling and turquoise accents scattered about the room amp up the wow factor. A Lucite coffee table, seagrass rug, and sensually curved seating all nod to timeless elegance.

Facing Page: Bands of white and black paint stretch through the home office, creating a distinct feeling in the space—it's artistic and unexpected. I emphasized the mustard yellow as the single accent color and paired a chair in the same tone with a curvy, high-gloss desk. The tall ceiling recesses even further thanks to its dark color. With so many windows I was able to combine contrasting bold patterns of white and black without overwhelming the room.
Photographs by Julia Lehman-McTigue

Jodi Macklin Interior Design

Maryland

Jodi Macklin enjoys creating spaces that suit the homeowners' lifestyles while providing them with a graceful harmony in both form and function. Subdued elegance, luxurious textures, and dynamic ambience characterize Jodi's designs. They embody a versatility that makes them the perfect places for intimate exchanges or entertaining a large party. With a keen eye for color, contrast, and texture—both visual and tangible—Jodi includes distinctive pieces in her projects while integrating the homeowners' personal style and needs to bring a room together. Luxury meets livable in Jodi's designs, as she fills rooms with warm comfort that invites guests to linger and enjoy.

Left: Built in the late 1700s, the Georgetown home is owned by a couple that loves to entertain. Its beauty speaks for itself, so I simply enhanced the original wood-paneled room with calming colors. Patterns in the mocha-colored mica coffee table and the blue-grey and cream carpet lend a traditional element to the historic home, while the simple lines in the furnishings remain true to the modern preferences of the homeowners.
Photograph by Gordon Beall

Above & Facing Page Top: The bright bedroom is flooded with natural light, creating an ethereal feeling. Neutral tones allow the room to appear delicate without looking overly feminine. A secluded owners' sanctuary, the bedroom includes a sitting area in warm grey tones for reading or relaxed conversation.

Facing Page Bottom: I enhanced the dining room's round table, which seats up to 12, by placing a curved buffet along the wall. Situated below a mirror with a modern wood frame, the buffet's elegance and clean lines help to unify the homeowners' love of traditional and modern design elements.
Photographs by Gordon Beall

"There needs to be a balance in design that creates a space that feels neither sparse nor cluttered." *Jodi Macklin*

Top: The dining room houses two square tables that can be used separately or together to seat up to 16 people. Comfortable upholstered chairs invite guests to linger after long dinners.

Bottom: A soothing color palette endows the home with a welcoming ambience. Layers of textures keep the bedroom looking soft and comfortable while remaining crisp and clean. In various shades of blues and creams, the bedroom is a relaxing retreat.

Facing Page: The kitchen is part of the home's family room, so I created a design that accommodates groups both large and small. Family and friends fit comfortably at the linear table, which is crowned with an elegant chandelier hung close to the coffered ceiling, keeping the view unobstructed.
Photographs by Gordon Beall

Kathryn Scott Design Studio

New York

Kathryn Scott has a fascination with a variety of styles, from historical architecture to modern design. She believes that integrating both new and old into a space provides a sense of timelessness and continuation, which is a beautiful way to create a dynamic environment. Her focus is crafting living spaces that provide the homeowners with something comfortable while allowing them to push their own boundaries with design. By looking beyond the design process and focusing on organization and problem solving, her projects result in long-lasting designs that keep homeowners comfortable from one decade to the next.

Left: With a view of the ocean, the living room is designed to feel relaxing and inviting—a person can walk into the space with sandy feet and not have to worry about disturbing the ambience. The room has a certain earthiness to it thanks to the use of natural materials. For instance, the walls are all pigmented stucco—not paint—and the floor is Mexican tile. Some of the tiles, which were installed in a pathway across the floor, even have little paw prints as a result of when a dog walked across them in the middle of the manufacturing process.
Photograph by Daniel Newcomb

"Design work essentially uses the same elements as creating art: balance, color, line, proportion, and composition." *Kathryn Scott*

Above: The homeowners enjoyed the process of collecting art for the house, including the wall sculpture in the bedroom. Its organic nature adds to the serene and reposeful environment, without detracting from the ocean vista that's visible from the bedroom's terrace.

Right: Situated between the dining room and the living room, the wet bar provides a place for guests to mingle and enjoy the view. In addition, the windows open up widely so drinks can be passed back and forth between the bar and the swimming pool area beyond.

Facing Page Top: The library mezzanine overlooks the living room and also shares a view of the ocean. The open area is bright, making it comfortable for reading, and the skylight above the nearby hallway creates the perfect light. The bright blue wall of the shelving niche provides an interesting pop of color to the natural-toned environment.

Facing Page Bottom: The home's relaxed, earthy feel continues into the dining area, which features a shared fireplace with the living room. A wrought iron lighting fixture provides an interesting visual element, especially in contrast with the large cypress ceiling beams.
Photographs by Daniel Newcomb

Laura Stein Interiors

Ontario

As a graphic designer and art director at a publishing company, Laura Stein reveled in designing sets for photo shoots. However there always seemed to be something missing: Beautiful rooms designed for a shoot remained two-dimensional and people couldn't interact with the images. Then a move back home to Toronto offered an opportunity to change careers. There she worked for HGTV and added design school to her resume. In 2006, Laura opened her firm, Laura Stein Interiors. Her diverse design background gives her a unique eye for a room's ensemble where textures, hues, lighting, and layers come together in an often unexpected way. Her love of travel and careful study of architectural and design history inform her work. She is continually looking for ways to bring classic design elements into the present. By combining traditional patterns with modern colors, linear furnishings with treasured keepsakes, Laura's classic-contemporary designs are utterly timeless.

Left: A contemporary take on Art Deco, the luxurious living room was created for a newly married couple who wanted a sophisticated design they could take with them to a larger home years later. Straight, angular lines play off the circles and soft curves that are repeated throughout the space. Lush silk drapery, custom velvet upholstery, walnut show wood, and sparkling chrome combine to create a glamorous atmosphere. The space is unified by a neutral color palette of warm grey and cream, accented with bold acid yellow. The look will transform easily with a simple change in accent color if the couple decides to move and separate the furniture into individual rooms.
Photograph by David Bagosy

Above & Right: The mandate for the master bedroom was understated luxury. The homeowners wanted it to be cozy, not fussy. With a comfortable sitting area to relax in, it's the perfect place for some much needed respite. The bedroom fills with light that filters through luxurious draperies. The L-shaped room provided the opportunity to design a library-like sitting area. Hardwood replaced the carpet flooring, and crown and panel moulding was added to the walls. Feminine softness is grounded by the masculine features inherent in the deep, rich wood tones. Bespoke pillows, custom bookshelves, and keepsakes from the owners' travels make the room an intimate and multifunctional retreat.
Photographs by David Bagosy

Facing Page: For their established home, the homeowners were looking for an updated mix of traditional and contemporary style. They wanted to keep their art collection and the bold rug in the room—everything else could go. The rug therefore informed the color palette: bright pink, soft blue, black, and white. Wingback chairs mingle with the linear sofa and angular chairs. Juxtaposed with sharper lines, the distinctly curvilinear silhouettes of the accent furniture seem playful. Classic patterns in bright colors make the room a fresh, welcoming update to the home.
Photographs by Mike Chajecki

Leyden Lewis Design Studio

New York

Leyden Lewis isn't content to consider interior design superficial. He believes a home's interiors act as backdrops to the stage of life, and manipulates those spaces accordingly to create places that resonate with their inhabitants. He seeks to combine surface—color and pattern—with space to depict cinematic as well as emotional landscapes. Primarily residential, Leyden Lewis Design Studio represents the culmination of Leyden's interior design and architectural training at Parsons. His Caribbean heritage, urban sophistication, and classical European modernism aesthetic make him one of New York's most celebrated designers. Surface, color, light, texture, and comfort dominate in Leyden's residences, which function as subtle retreats that elicit visceral reactions.

Left: Most rooms are square; I love to soften that up by setting up curves and diagonals using dynamic furniture shapes and arrangements. The casual living room, grounded by a Malene B rug inspired by the Caribbean Sea, contains a mirrored coffee table from the 1940s, an antler horn mirror, rounded slipper chairs, and a set of framed Tony Whitfield photographic art pieces. As an artist and a collector myself, I consider contemporary art more than decoration, and it's important for me to use it throughout my work.
Photograph by Eric Hernandez

Above: Mechanical reasons had necessitated the dropping of an urban apartment's entry foyer ceiling at the perimeter. The solution: a light fixture with a skylight feel to keep the visual weight off and the ephemeral in. Long-term collections converge, as a contemporary Afghani rug sits next to a French sugar cabinet from the 1930s, now employed as a holder of gloves and hats. The foyer adjoins the area designated as "office" in the living room, where a writing table occupies one corner; the transparent effect of glass keeps the space feeling open. Low, open-armed chairs and round tables form a dynamic arrangement within the room and resist the conventions of the given angles of the space.
Photographs by Pate Eng

Right: In contrast to the warm colors in the living room, we brought soothing sage walls and cream-carpeting for serenity into the bedroom. A 1950s night table and an acrylic Plexiglas-framed mirror atop a Korean tansu chest flank the bed.
Photograph by Pate Eng

Facing Page Top: The homeowners sought an elegant, urban quality in their artsy, affluent Pennsylvania suburban home. Vintage pieces collected from the area's notable art and antique shops give the rooms local flair. In the main dining area, I paired a Modern classic, the marble-topped Saarinen table, with a high-backed bench for warmth, and painted a whimsical rustling tree complete with birds in matte gold and blue on the wall. "Smoked oyster" was the color selected for the walls and sheer curtains framing the master bedroom vanity, bringing a much-needed sense of chic.
Photographs by Eric Hernandez

Facing Page Bottom: To anchor a large wall in the apartment and complement big expanses of color elsewhere, we organized and framed an assemblage of photos from the homeowners' trip to the Galapagos Islands. A round wool area rug keeps the rotation flowing, as does the circular coffee table and the boomerang-shaped sofa in a persimmon hue.
Photograph by Pate Eng

Lilly Levy Designs

New Jersey

Lilly Levy knows what her homeowners want. Years spent as an apparel buyer for her family's clothing stores taught her how to zero in on color, style, and trends in a way that most people spend a career trying to master. After bolstering her instincts with a degree from New York School of Interior Design in 1998, Lilly launched her eponymous design firm and has spent the years since helping to transform design dreams into livable spaces. Armed with a keen intuition toward architecture and construction, Lilly also builds about eight houses a year herself, dialing in on the angles, colors, and practical concerns that make her properties and designs unforgettable.

Left: Shapes are the building blocks of strong design work. The geometry of the wood and marble floor, the silver geometric wallpaper, and the architectural steel staircase cooperate in a way that is both cohesive and surprising.
Photograph by John Neitzel

Above: Striking hues of eggplant and chartreuse converge to elevate the master bedroom from surprising to extraordinary. Like a lush cocoon of color, the room provides a perfect space for cozying in and winding down. Zoffany wallpapers and fabrics are so textural and lush. I love to layer them in with custom-made pieces, like the side tables that I constructed myself. Add a couple Murano glass lamps, a purple vinyl daybed, and zebra tonal carpet, and the space takes on a life of its own.

Facing Page Top: A geometric marble floor is so striking that the rest of the room just needs to follow its lead. The pattern is mirrored in the modern wood wall moulding. We balanced the massive dining table by hanging two chandeliers, which play off each other beautifully. The shimmery paint on the walls and ceiling further amplifies the glamour.

Facing Page Bottom: Gemstone trim tiles and a Christopher Guy mirror in the powder room add to the home's glittering, dressy feel. A pair of armoires that I designed in anigre wood with crystal handles flanks the dining room windows.
Photographs by John Neitzel

"A designer must be driven to understand her homeowners but also to push them past what was thought possible." *Lilly Levy*

Lori Shinal Interiors

Pennsylvania

Artists find inspiration in the world around them and for Lori Shinal, inspiration comes to her while traveling the world. Her career in Ralph Lauren's home collection department gave her the foundation her firm, Lori Shinal Interiors, is built on. Her subsequent exposure to different cultural influences fuels her creativity, and love for design and creating welcoming spaces. Through her partnership with Barney's New York, Lori's decorative pieces are accessible to homeowners across the nation. Her designs are characterized by the attention to detail that goes into each surface of the room; everything from floor to ceiling is considered and becomes part of the overall design. Rooms touched by Lori's artistry, in collaboration with her invaluable assistant Megan Matthews, are specifically conducive to the homeowners' lifestyle. Her own family provides inspiration to create rooms that welcome adults and children alike. With a belief that homes reflect the life experiences, travels, and memories of her clientele, Lori makes each space unforgettable.

Left: In a room where rich navy sofas become the neutral pieces, timeless meets edgy in a completely new way. The homeowners were pleased to take the risk of black textured wallpaper when I proposed the living room's design. The pair of navy blue sofas was custom made for the space and the velvet texture creates a contrast with the matte fireplace surround. The pillows make a statement with a bold graphic pattern and the shimmer of the gold shelves perfectly showcases a unique collection of accessories.
Photograph by Joanne Posse

Above: I worked with two amazing decorative painters—Meg Shattuck and John Ferris—to create the Venetian plaster walls and ceiling in the grand family room. The homeowner visited the studio where the sectional was being custom built. It's the most comfortable sectional; you want to sink right into it. A marble and wood coffee table and a long daybed behind the sectional that looks out onto the lawn were other custom elements specific to the space. Citron accents play off the blue, and I love to add vibrancy with pops of red.

Right: At the foot of the grand staircase, the luxurious sitting area feels like an intimate jewel box with unique wallcovering made from string. Romantic elements like the velvet ombre sofa and the coffee table are perfectly positioned in the streamlined space, which is stylish and smart without being too ornate.

Facing Page Top Left: Entryways introduce the entire tone of a home. Light floods the previously dark space and elements such as the marble floor and ornate, hand-forged, wrought iron front door are juxtaposed with a large-scale flocked wallcovering in a modern floral design. The combination of dark and light allows for the wainscoting, windows, and doorway to stand out and receive the attention they deserve.

Facing Page Top Right: Vibrant green walls and a dark brick floor come together in the entryway to create a modern cottage feel. Light filters in through the beautiful transom windows and illuminates the space. A heavy, lyre-base console table sits under shimmery wall sconces and a delicate mirror, creating an ideal balance of style.

Facing Page Bottom: The graceful lines of the canopy bed mimic the curves in the ceiling above, drawing the eye upward. It fills the vertical space well without being too heavy. Soft tones and luxurious bed linens make the master bedroom a relaxing retreat.
Photographs by Joanne Posse

Patricia Gorman Associates

Pennsylvania

From renovating historic homes to designing prestigious vacation retreats across the country, Trish Gorman has made it her business to bring reality to homeowners' visions. Since founding Patricia Gorman Associates in 1985, she has worked closely with architects, builders, contractors, and vendors to create truly unique homes to such great popularity that the firm has subsequently expanded to include a secondary headquarters in Aspen, Colorado. A design boutique, DIGS, specializing in upscale and antique furniture and accessories, rounds out the business. Sourcing materials from Europe, Asia, and the Middle East, boldly expanding floorplans, and carefully installing prized collections, Trish and her team work hand-in-hand with homeowners from the first floorboard to the last finishing touch.

Left: The Stone Mountain kitchen renovation in Villanova, Pennsylvania, was a challenging project: we had to expand the existing structure to make room for the modern kitchen. A back entry, mudroom, coat closet, desk area, and breakfast room were all added to the space, which connects to the existing family room. A thick, dark-stained wood countertop on the island gives the room a rustic feel against the surrounding granite-topped, furniture-style cabinets. A green beadboard nook in the island is perfect for accessories or cookbooks. The impressive copper hood over the stainless commercial oven stands out against the cream millwork.
Photograph courtesy of Patricia Gorman Associates

"Treat one-of-a-kind materials with a reverence that shows in the final design." *Trish Gorman*

Above & Right: Built on a 12-acre peninsula in the small fishing town of Rock Hall, Maryland, the classical Arts-and-Crafts style home was designed to be a retreat for family and friends. The connected main structure and guesthouse were built to maximize stunning views of the water. The stairway in the two-story living room directs the eye to the exposed timbers and lighthouse cupola above. Throughout the house, neutral furnishings are oriented toward the windows so that guests can wake up to the beautiful panorama outside.

Facing Page: Comfortable luxury embraces every room of the Aspen, Colorado, home, which includes pieces brought in from Paris, Israel, India, and elsewhere in Asia. Stunning vaulted ceilings, antique fireplaces and mantels, and reclaimed stone flooring, which once served as streets in Jerusalem, elevate the drama of the Tuscan-style farmhouse. Over the four and a half years it took to complete, we approached the project with great respect for each of the unique materials used to make the estate an Old World dream for the owners.
Photographs courtesy of Patricia Gorman Associates

The Patterson Group

Massachusetts

Eileen Patterson garners inspiration from the bones of a home—the existing architecture that defines a room. A gifted designer who does both interior design and architectural design, Patterson works with the homeowner to create inspired living areas, full of balance, rhythm, color, and scale. It is an understanding of traditional art technique that encourages Eileen to explore large-scale and intensive design projects. By combining a mix of materials, such as metal, marble, wood, stone, and crystal, with an elegant color palette, even her most contemporary layouts hold onto their modernity for decades to follow. Each project displays flawless refinement and a timeless design.

Left: Designed to make a stunning first impression, the foyer is an exquisitely detailed yet highly useable space. To provide the homeowner with the utmost privacy, I designed two sets of double doors: The exterior set is glass and iron, while the interior doors are bleached and pickled rift sawn white oak. When closed, the interior oak doors add privacy while maintaining the room's seamless design. Wanting to highlight the elliptical shape of the foyer, I personally designed the artwork, which is a 1930s-style raw plaster and silver leaf bas relief that follows the contour of the wall. The curved staircase railing is solid nickel, a rare application of this rigid material. An original 1930s silvered and crystal chandelier hangs overhead.
Photographs by Michael J. Lee

"Traditional design with a twist is something that will still look great in 15 years." *Eileen Patterson*

Above: The atrium serves two purposes: an area for relaxation and a space to entertain more guests than the dining room would accommodate. I custom-designed a pair of tables and sideboards that can be combined to form one long seating space. Blocks of limestone comprise the walls while the ceiling features a distinguishing design element: bleached and pickled wood planks with beveled edges. The luxe powder room features a subtle taupe-toned vanity and leather walls accented with nickel.

Facing Page: The dining room was the very first area designed in the home, and the room's artwork served as my inspiration. The design features 20th-century wall panels, each individually installed on a silver leaf wall; the nearby curved niches are also silver leaf. A nickel and crystal chandelier is reflected above the high-gloss dining table. Lemon yellow tones were used for the 1930s-style dining chairs and Tibetan hand-woven rug.
Photographs by Michael J. Lee

Above & Right: I wanted to avoid a "typical" kitchen look, and instead aimed for the appearance of a 20th-century living space. Selecting unique cabinetry and furniture, as well as splitting up the space into a kitchen and banquette area, helps accomplish this. The banquette boasts serene hues and overlooks the property's lush gardens.

Facing Page: The open living room, which features striking red-orange walls with a high-gloss finish, looks out into the adjoining atrium. I incorporated inlaid nickel into the doors and handles, which complement the finishes used throughout the design. Doors leading into a built-in bar borrow the same bright red-orange gloss finish.
Photographs by Michael J. Lee

Right & Below: I designed the dressing area to encompass all the necessities while maintaining the essence of glamour. The mirror pays homage to the large 1920s-style vanities, and the soft blue tones on the cabinet and built-in chest lend the room elegant tranquility. To match the classic 1920s ambience, the home's library and office feature nickel banding and fabric styles often used in the era.

Facing Page: The master suite is both a bedroom and spa-like retreat. Lounge chairs and an ottoman create a comfortable sitting area. The walls, headboard, and built-in cabinetry, which are covered in a soft-blue Ultrasuede, further the serenity. A large armoire in dark wood provides a focal point in the space; its doors are covered in soft cream leather, accented with nickel. The luminous master bath features a white glass double-vanity with nickel details and custom stainless steel and crystal sconces. Gradated frosted glass encloses the shower.
Photographs by Michael J. Lee

Sagart Studio

Washington, D.C.

Straightforward, instinctive, cosmopolitan interior architecture and design defines the portfolio of Vincent Sagart. Often blending styles and influences in pursuit of livable luxury, Vincent designs spaces that are livable and luxurious at once. Growing up in Europe, Vincent spent his childhood surrounded by creative minds, apprenticing for well-known artists and discovering his affection for art and design early on. He went on to receive master's degrees in computer-aided design and stage and costume design. After a successful career in theater and design in Europe, Vincent moved his practice to Washington, D.C., and in 1999 launched a full-service design studio and showroom with his artist wife, Helena. Today their showroom represents European manufacturers of kitchens, dressing rooms, cabinetry, lighting, and bath products. To share his passion for arts and design, he also lectured for more than a decade as an adjunct professor at Marymount University.

Left: The master bath was designed to bring together two elements of nature: light and water. The carrara marble shower underscores the purity of the space. Furnished only with a rough-surfaced cedar wood stool and sculptural shelf to store bathing essentials, the shower emulates the elements of the earth together in one soothing space.
Photograph by Sagart Studio

Above & Facing Page Left: The Orange County, Virginia, home was in disrepair when the project began. The solution was to demolish most of the interior walls and create pristine spaces while preserving the character of the home. The reappointed space represents my design philosophy of openness accompanied by lightness and flexibility. The contemporary lines complement the local fieldstone fireplace, integrating modern European design sensibilities with the immediate location of the home. A blend of country traditionalist and minimalist contemporary, the clean-lined kitchen opens to the living room. Each space is illuminated with natural and artificial light.

Facing Page Right: Subdued colors and natural light create a place of respite in the guest bedroom while artwork and accessories pay homage to Virginia's equestrian legacy.
Photographs by Sagart Studio

Willey Design

New York

Having photos of your very first solo project published in a magazine would be a good omen for any designer. But when the designer is as motivated and promising as John Willey, the lacquered sky is the limit. As sought after for his Brentwood bungalows as he is for his Central Park pied-á-terres, John's designs explode in directions that are simultaneously provocative and chic without ever feeling too precious. His natural talent for finding inspiration in unexpected places, his meticulous attention to detail and his pedigree from Chicago's International Academy of Design have combined to earn him a solid following and a reputation for magical transformations.

Left: When a New York City townhouse needed a transformation, I was proud to retain the 100-year-old charm while giving it a youthful lift. I created a combined dining and living room with a corner seating area to provide multiple uses for today's family. The walls are combed and tinted plaster and set against a sky-blue ceiling. Cream velvet upholstery, geometric patterns, and a delicious grey and blue rug complement a striking cluster globe chandelier, modern art, and unexpected vintage elements. The quietly luxurious room evokes a calm and sensible elegance.
Photograph by Robert Granoff

Above: For the residence on Manhattan's Upper East Side, I revamped the 30-foot-long drawing room with bright spots of aubergine, cream, and pale blue to provide playful elements throughout. The pale green wool drapes and custom chocolate brown trellis rug add texture and a wonderful base of color. In the evening, reflected light from the taxicabs driving up Madison Avenue flickers against the lacquered ceiling and the effect is absolutely magical.
Photograph by David Jacquot

Right & Facing Page: To create more living space in a five-bedroom pied-á-terre in New York's iconic 15 Central Park West building, we poached two walk-in closets and one bedroom to create a library with a 14-foot custom sofa. Black lacquer bookcases backed with antique mirrors line the wall, while bleached floors and ribbed grasscloth wallpaper ensure that the space doesn't get too serious. In the foyer, we imported three hand-blown, mercury glass fixtures from France, then lined the space with antique mirrors, lacquered the ceilings, and added Regency detailing to create a French-inspired space with an energized, modern twist.
Photographs by David Jacquot

"To keep a room from getting too precious, combine high-impact items with humble materials." *John Willey*

Above: A pale blue velvet headboard softens the lines of the master suite's custom, bleached-oak bed. We trimmed a chenille wall panel with nickel studs and added a Moroccan-inspired silk carpet, which feels fantastic underfoot. The bedside lamps, shaded in linen with gray piping, are based on a 1940s French suspended light by Paul Dupré-Lafon. Parchment-covered side tables from Holly Hunt add functional beauty.
Photograph by David Jacquot

Facing Page Top: We moved the breakfast room and kitchen in a Sag Harbor lakefront home from one end of the home to the other. Now the bright and sporty room is home to a custom banquette and driftwood table, and has direct access to the waterfront and pool area. Blue lacquered chairs by Hans Wegner add a happy, calming energy. The woven rattan chandelier was an impulse buy; we spotted it in a shop in the Hamptons and bought it on the spot.
Photograph by Scott Fisher

Bottom Left: To create a quiet yet engaging foyer in a Chappaqua residence, we brought in a gold-leaf chandelier with parchment shades that mimics a lily pad. We also introduced a stately pedestal table and a silk rug in chocolate brown and ivory. Double-height windows enhance the drama by offering expansive views of the property beyond.
Photograph by John Willey

Bottom right: A faceted, polished-oak cabinet from Therien Studios is as functional as it is sculptural in an Upper West Side residence's media room. The colored glass cubes in the corner light by George Kovacs can be rearranged to suit the owner's style and lighting needs.
Photograph by David Jacquot

Adams Design, Inc.

Washington, D.C.

Compelled to attend design school after a successful career in New York and on Capitol Hill, Lisa Adams, founder of Adams Design, Inc., uses her unparalleled educational background to inform her creativity. With degrees from Yale, Columbia, and Mount Vernon College—now part of George Washington University—Lisa draws on her knowledge from her professional degrees to set the parameters of her designs, which are planned to every detail. Lisa's projects are characterized by her attention to the structure of a space, enhanced by an organic feel. Earthbound solids, rays of light extending inward from the outside world, and natural fabrics are typical elements of her designs. Each room also promotes the architecture of the home, showcasing the beautiful underlying scheme from which Lisa derives her inspiration.

Left: Nature inspired my design in the living room of a DC metropolitan area residence designed by architect Alan Dynerman of Dynerman Architects PC. The view of the landscape is an important feature of the room, enhanced by the wood finishes, stone walls, and slate floors. A custom Odegard rug features an organic pattern, mimicked by the curve of the furniture. I worked with the architect and the homeowners to create a functional space for a large family that complemented the design of the home. The result is an intimate grouping that allows for cozy conversation.
Photograph by Paul Burk Photography

"Design should reflect the homeowner, be right for the architecture, and withstand the test of time." *Lisa Adams*

Above: Traditional in concept and modern in style, the dining room features a custom designed table that was made from a single slab of figured walnut and seats up to 22 people. The custom chandelier was inspired by the homeowners' trip to Murano, Italy, and is constructed from 21 cones of hand-blown glass in tones of blue and brown. Stretching under the long table, the rug complements the one found in the living room.

Facing Page Top & Bottom: Two seating areas are united by the custom rug that gives the room a vibrant pop of color. Less formal than the living room, the space boasts organic furniture such as the coffee table and teak root end tables, and durable upholstery that endures the effects of large parties and small children. The stone fireplace brings warmth to the space, and the smaller scale grouping nearby draws the size of the room down to a more intimate space.
Photographs by Paul Burk Photography

Above: Flexible in form and function, the enclosed porch is where the indoors meet the outside world. I selected the teak furniture to complement the mahogany architecture, giving the space a two-toned palette. To increase the versatility of the space, the sectional can be rearranged and moved for different events and the two long dining tables can be used separately or together for informal dining. Large sliding doors open to the adjacent pool area, making it the perfect place to entertain family and friends.

Left: Quilted makore wood, linear bookshelves, and small piercings of light through the windows combine to create an intimate, private space for study and reflection. I really wanted the architecture of the room to dominate the space. The dark wood tones, bright rug, and traditional seating area make it an adult, tailored space for the intellectual and well-traveled homeowners.
Photographs by Paul Burk Photography

Amanda Maier Design

Pennsylvania

Amanda Maier loves to design rooms that others will love and appreciate, spaces that homeowners will enjoy for years to come. When she founded Amanda Maier Design in 2007, Amanda combined her traveling experiences and the knowledge gained at the Art Institute of Philadelphia, along with several years of experience in high-end residential design, to create her dream. Her experiences, along with a natural talent for design, allow Amanda to create rooms that are a unique combination of sparkle and modernism. Her keen eye for detail results in spaces that come together seamlessly and never look cluttered. Her bold personality guarantees something completely unexpected in every room. By combining contrasting elements—mismatched hardwoods, mid-century chairs, glamorous glass tile—Amanda creates stunning rooms that are beautifully timeless.

Left: I tend to fall in love with my projects—each one is my new favorite—but the contemporary dining room always ranks as one of my beloved designs. It was very dark to begin with and the homeowners not only wanted to brighten it up, they also wanted to combine rustic and glitzy elements in the design. The wainscoting received a modern twist with color inserts that match the shade painted on the ceiling. Metallic trees adorn the wallcovering and its hint of shimmer gives a luminescence to the room. The host and hostess chairs on either end of the large table embody the tone of the room: the modern citron fabric attached with nailhead trim is the perfect mix of classic and modern.
Photograph by Damon Landry

"Design is so versatile. It's always changing and evolving." *Amanda Maier*

Above: The homeowners frequently entertain, so I had to work numerous appliances into the plan: three sinks, a bar refrigerator, a wine refrigerator, and an industrial range. Dark cherry and burled maple cabinets offset the vibrant colors of the kitchen. Highly durable, eco-friendly cork floors give the room a casual but elegant feel while remaining comfortable underfoot. Absolutely every detail of the room was important, from how the butcher block integrated with the granite island top to the subtle textured glass on the upper cabinets.

Facing Page Top Left: Even a bachelor's bathroom needs a bit of the feminine to balance it out. Embracing a touch of glam, I created a modern bathroom that speaks to the homeowner's sophistication. The mirror's retro attitude and modernized Rococo style, the off-set sink that allows for more counter space, and the band of tile that tracks across the room behind the mirror make the room artful in addition to functional.

Facing Page Top Right: I transformed an awkward closet into a wet-bar off the dining room. The custom designed wave sink made from recycled concrete needed hydraulic lifts to install it in its floating position. The sculptural faucet and slate-and-glass tile make it an intriguing element of the room.

Facing Page Bottom Left: I love creating a spa-like atmosphere in bathrooms. Natural elements including the shower panel with reeds embedded in the glass and organic slate-like porcelain floors come together in a room that's universally accessible without looking like it. With a showerhead mounted directly on the glass, the enclosure seems to disappear and the room remains open and peaceful.

Facing Page Bottom Right: Modern metallic wallpaper extended onto the ceiling turns the powder room into a little jewel box. A hammered nickel mirror, sconces made from LED-lit chunks of crystal, and glass mosaic tile with glass grout give the room the right amount of punch.
Photographs by Damon Landry

Calder Design Group

New York

To the team at Calder Design Group, interior design isn't just about arranging belongings within a room. It's about realizing the everyday needs and wants of their homeowners and translating those wishes into spaces that reflect a complete lifestyle. Discovering what makes homes function at their best—whether the ultimate goal is relaxation or a home that encourages entertaining—is only the starting point for the designers. By seeking out inspiration in everything from boutique hotels to far-flung destinations to films, founder Nicholas, daughter Melanie, and their talented team are able to introduce elements that elevate everyday solutions into beautiful, functional designs.

Left: Exhibiting the softer side of contemporary design, the bar area and butler's pantry utilizes natural wood with a soothing horizontal grain and a pebbled floor for added texture. One of my signature ways to add a pop of color is to fill pretty jars with water and a few drops of food coloring. There's no easier way to freshen up a room or introduce a new color than by emptying and refilling a vase.
Photograph by Joshua Hughes

"Inspiration is everywhere. You can find something to be inspired by halfway around the world or even just down the street."
Nicholas Calder

Above & Facing Page: I designed the kitchen around the idea of "industrial chic," with an abundance of natural stone to contribute depth and color variation. Shinnoki cabinetry and a raked oak table establish an organic atmosphere, which is furthered by a divider made of fine chainmail that resembles a delicate sheet of rain.
Photographs by Joshua Hughes

Justin Shaulis

New York

Whether he's designing the interiors of a hip new restaurant, a healthcare office, or a distinctive home, Justin Shaulis' main focus is the emotive design element of the space. Since founding his firm in 2002, Justin has brought homeowners a boutique-style philosophy to design—it's a highly specialized, personal, holistic approach to improving a homeowner's surroundings. As an HGTV designer featured on the show "Home Rules," Justin has worked to remove the chaos of disorder from the lives of homeowners, and it is something he's been passionate about since entering the industry. With a distinctive eye for juxtaposed styles and cultural diversity, Justin's creations are bold yet refined, striking and welcoming all at once.

Left: The living room, with its beautiful views of the city, was designed with entertaining and conversation in mind. Multiple vignettes composed of various textures, fabrics, and forms of seating convey warmth in the open space. Area rugs ground the furniture arrangements. Handpainted acrylic panels top the coffee table and a retro sofa with purple pillows adds a mid-century modern twist to an otherwise classic space.
Photograph by Beth Bates

"Texture not only defines a space, it also sets the mood of the room and affects how people feel in it." *Justin Shaulis*

Above: I let the brick wall become the focal point of the dining space in the otherwise sleek Chelsea loft. It gives texture to the room and balances the grey stone of the kitchen countertops.

Facing Page Top: A low-profile oversized sectional provides ample seating in the loft's living room. The rectilinear space is balanced by the diagonally installed hardwood floor, which draws the eye to the view.

Facing Page Bottom: Abundant natural light filters into the peaceful bedroom. Custom Amish-built furnishings and grasscloth wallcovering grant the room a warm organic element that's simple and elegant.
Photographs by Marko MacPherson

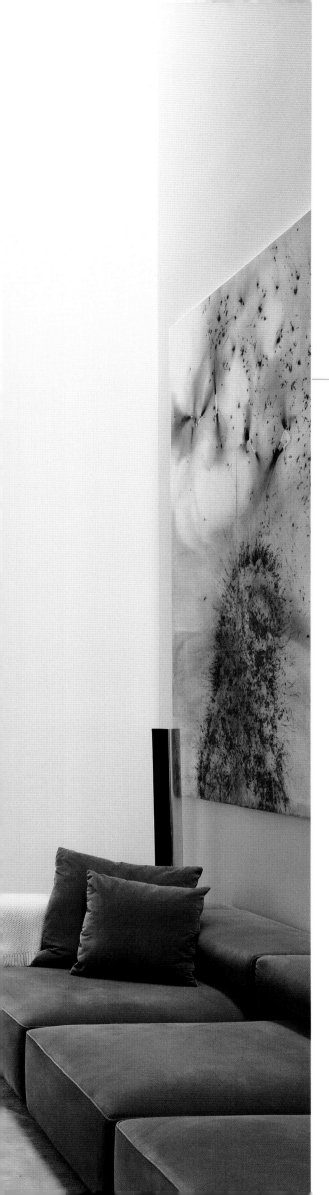

Kathryn Scott Design Studio

New York

Kathryn Scott composes her designs by first envisioning a homeowner's particular lifestyle, then moving backwards to transform that vision into reality. It's this transformation—from concept into composition—that inspires Kathryn to create clean, comfortable, and highly livable environments. She began her career by viewing rooms as a work of art, focusing on balance and proportion to create stunning layouts, which she then fills with an intricate attention to detail. With her appreciation for even the smallest components, the layouts she creates are devoid of mass-produced design elements and are instead imbued with personality and creativity.

Left: A peculiar architectural trait of the house is that it's situated in the countryside surrounded by the beautiful landscape—but there are not many large windows to focus on the view. Instead, windows are placed to sculpt the light as it shines in and illuminates the art collection, becoming a living part of the design itself. The home was designed by the collaboration of Ai Weiwei and architect Simon Frommenwiler, of Switzerland-based HHF Architects. *Photograph by Nicholas Koenig*

Above: The home office is as serene and peaceful as the rest of the house; its smooth lines and uncluttered aesthetic help achieve that. The entire residence is treated as a sculptural piece by keeping the furnishings minimal.

Right Top & Bottom: Each room features a few pieces of sculptural furniture that are works of art in themselves. To add a pop of color in the master bedroom, a red dinosaur—a contemporary art piece by Jiango Sui—stands guard in the corner. The guest room bed linen is a wool felt, made with a striking handmade texture.

Facing Page Top: It was essential to highlight the homeowners' collection of Chinese contemporary art, and the dining room does just that. An Asian-inspired dining table with a single bench on each side of the table serves as the perfect complement to the art piece above it.

Facing Page Bottom Left: The foyer not only serves as the introduction for the homeowners' contemporary art pieces, but as soon as guests enter the home, they immediately get the feeling for its open, fresh, and airy room qualities.

Facing Page Bottom Right: With its minimalist design, the kitchen doesn't distract from the home's overall sense of serenity. The intimate dining area features larger scale chairs for comfort and a soft touch of drama.
Photographs by Ellen McDermott

Marie Burgos Design

New York

When approaching a design, Marie Burgos doesn't invade the space, but rather uses the philosophy of Feng-Shui to create a harmonious design that plays into its present character. Her projects focus on the balance of space and objects, bringing the five forces of nature into a home: water, wood, fire, earth, and metal. She often employs a *bagua*, or energy map, to determine what characteristics each area of square footage promotes, such as career, love, or family. By keeping in tune with a room's architecture and the homeowner's unique vision, Marie creates elegant environments that spotlight subtle differences in material, shape, color, and light. Her designs develop a skillful equilibrium between function and form.

Left: Designed to accommodate an upscale Manhattan lifestyle, the space provides the homeowner with separate environments for entertaining, relaxing, and working. The building was originally a spice warehouse, and I wanted to keep the original Old World elegance offered by the architecture. I achieved this by combining neutral, modern finishes—such as the oak floors and white walls with a lot of texture—with an interesting collection of fabrics, from cotton to cowhide. In the center of the living space, a one-of-a-kind Indonesian wooden block coffee table sits atop a hand-loomed twill stripe jute rug. By combining rustic elements and modern pieces, I was able to maintain the character of the 18th-century space.
Photograph by Francis Augustine

Above: The living area's reading nook features several rustic pieces re-imagined for modern times. An Eames lounge chair and matching ottoman in white leather are placed upon a cowhide rug, and the side table is a traditional milking stool, but with a modern twist: mango wood tripod legs and an aluminum top. An acrylic fine art piece by Francis Augustine titled "Cappuccino" casts warmth upon the space, a stunning complement to the New York City skyline.

Right: I borrowed inspiration from the building's existing features, such as the original brick walls, when creating the stately yet serene living environment. The exaggerated wall clock plays up the vintage aspects of the design, and the grey wood television stand with aluminum legs creates harmony between the Old World and modern conveniences.

Facing Page Top: A blend of iron and distressed mango wood gives the dining table an industrial aesthetic. The host and hostess wing chairs cap either end of the table and the solid oak dining chairs lend themselves to the dining area's French farmhouse appeal. I wanted to impart the building's character through the use of industrial design elements, such as the bronze-finished metal light pendant, a precise reproduction of an antique light from centuries ago. A floor mirror, made from vintage wooden planks salvaged from boats, rounds out the design.

Facing Page Bottom: A Marlo bed takes center stage in the master bedroom. The ambience is peaceful, yet remains influenced by the home's Old World feel, thanks to a contradiction of patterns and textures, such as the bed's Italian vintage Baroque bedding, a cowhide bench, flowing white linen drapes, and a geometric pattern Indian rug. Reflective surfaces bring in a touch of glamour, as seen in the antique convex mirror and the mercury glass bedside table lamps.
Photographs by Francis Augustine

Matthew Yee, Inc.

New York

Matthew Yee fell in love with the world of design through the clear lens of Lucite. A first job with Les Prismatiques gave him a taste of high-end Lucite furniture, a stint with Country Floors cut his teeth on tile and stone, and before long, tile-maven Ann Sacks tapped him to run her New York City operations. Along the way, the naturally social Matthew became the go-to confidante of architects, designers, and builders needing inspiration. So it was only natural that, 17 years in, when he decided to take a break and sell real estate, he was the one to whom the other brokers came to for advice on staging and renovating their properties. Word of mouth spread, his name was passed along, and soon Matthew Yee became recognized as the perfect crossover: an industry insider who knew real estate, materials, and had a natural flair for contemporary design that has made him a current favorite of everyone from city socialites to Long Island empty-nesters.

Left: In my home office, the floor-to-ceiling windows have the potential to make the space feel contemporary in a cold way, but I was intent on creating a homey feeling like I grew up with on Long Island. The antiques and Asian elements were handed down to me from my family, so I designed the apartment with each piece in mind. I purchased the Les Prismatiques Lucite coffee table when I was working with Ann Sacks and could finally afford the investment. Buying it was a real milestone for me. I love how light and airy it is and how it can swing from contemporary to classic depending on the accessories.
Photograph by Brett Beyer

Above & Right: A home on Sutton Place owned by a New York City socialite needed a whole new look. The owner was downsizing from a large townhouse full of heavy, ornate fixtures and antiques, but she was so youthful and vivacious that there was an obvious disconnect. She allowed me to design a space to match her personality while keeping some of the antique elements that speak to her history. She had never even heard of a cow hide rug or using Lucite for a coffee table, but she loved them. In the end, the contemporary damask curtains, animal print on the chairs, and limestone fireplace livened things up but kept the story true to the pre-war bones of the building.

Facing Page Top: The footprint of a Greenwich Village living room promised huge potential. The gentleman was moving to the city from Texas and was the only homeowner I ever worked with who said that he didn't like light. The challenge was to create a space that would be masculine and sexy but also fully functional and properly illuminated. In the end we hit on all marks, and the serene and sultry wall color thoroughly urbanized the displaced Texan.

Facing Page Bottom: A pair of empty nesters wanted to modernize their Central Park South apartment with a design that captured the views of the park's lush trees. The husband and wife were sporty, natural, casual people, but given the location the apartment had to retain an air of elegance. So we designed the space with their family in mind, using all new furnishings in greens and sand colors, and accented the ceiling with wrought iron lanterns with seeded glass for just enough sophistication. Light touches of Asiana paid homage to the wife's love of acupuncture and Chinese culture.
Photographs by Brett Beyer

Michael Shannon Designs

Pennsylvania

Whether it's a living room that needs to live up to its impressive views or a master bath in desperate need of modernization, Michael Shannon Designs always focuses on the wants and needs of the homeowner. With over three decades in the residential and commercial design industry, Michael's experience has fostered in him a broad understanding of the various facets of the trade. From interior architecture and the complete reconfiguration of existing spaces to interior decoration and the selection of furniture, fabrics, and finishes for a new home, Michael and his team work on full-service contracts as well as hourly consultation sessions. Because the firm's repertoire transcends the boundaries of standard design philosophies, such as traditional or modern, the result is a truly unique aesthetic personalized to each homeowner and their desires. With each new project, Michael Shannon Designs strives to create a beautiful, functional space for everyday living.

Left: It's hard to believe that the room once had shag carpeting, track lighting, curved walls, and mirrored furniture. When fate brought the husband and wife that call the 3,600-square-foot home to Michael Shannon Designs, the goal was to create a dramatic living environment that exuded comfort and sophistication while complementing their unobstructed Hudson River views. Architectural lighting accentuates the organic elements of the room. A raw edge walnut slab window seat showcases the homeowners' artistic creations and the floor lamps that flank the sofa could almost be mistaken for trees. The oversized custom sectional sofa is perfect for entertaining and the pair of lounge chairs in a pop of red are a nod to their love of mid-century design.
Photograph by Barry Halkin Photography

Above: Even the most organized people can agree that the office is often the one place in the home that gets unruly. The solution was custom millwork to house all of the unsightly accoutrements, a leather desk surface inlay for note drafting, and fabric wallcovering from floor to ceiling to keep it cozy. The room wouldn't be complete without an iconic piece of furniture for snuggling up with a good book at the end of a long day.

Left: Center stage in the room is a painting of "Cookie," the colorful monkey who holds a very special place in the homeowners' hearts. It served as the inspiration for the library and adjoining guest bedroom suites. Bold pops of color and the mix of patterns and prints make the rooms inviting. Most of the furniture in the library was inherited from the homeowners' parents. The 1950s era cocktail and end tables are right at home with the reupholstered club chairs.

Facing Page Top Left: We had the opportunity to design and build several architectural elements, such as the staircase and entry cabinetry, with local artisans. The waxed hickory stairs and hand-forged steel open railing are a design detail carried throughout the home that emphasizes the contemporary architecture. The custom cabinets are home to the many keepsakes, artifacts, and tchotchkes that the owners have accumulated during their travels throughout the years.

Facing Page Top Right: Simple, functional, and cozy are the words the homeowners used to describe their ideal bathroom. The design began with the selection of the tub—a crucial element for the owner's daily routine. It is ergonomic and stylish all at once. Maintaining the two areas as one, the shower tile was continued from floor to ceiling throughout, and an open-air shower was created with a full glass enclosure. The tile bench is the perfect balance of function and form and the roller shades provide the ease of privacy with a simple tug.
Photographs by Barry Halkin Photography

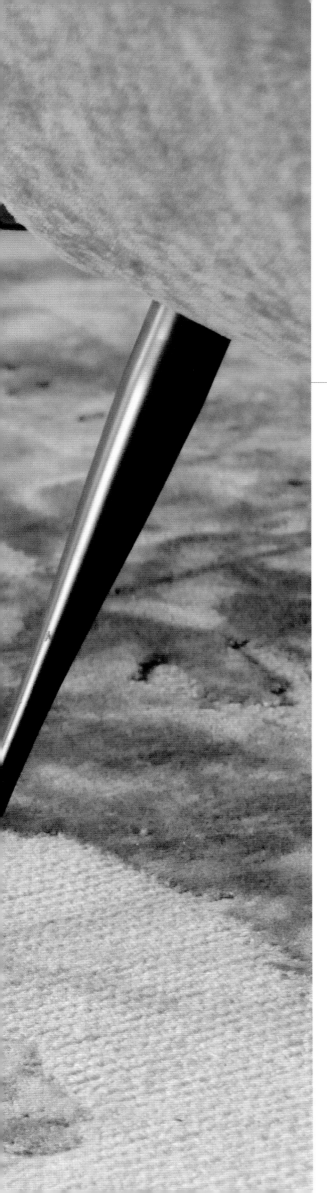

P&T Interiors

New York

Eclectic. Inventive. Unexpected. As hard to define as it is to emulate, P&T Interiors founder Pol G. Theis' approach to interior design mirrors the unique caliber of the projects he tackles. Since 2002, he and his P&T team have been working closely with homeowners to distill their innermost wishes before shaping them into residential reality. With a clientele that spans the globe, Pol allows his Parisian upbringing and New York worldliness to infuse his designs with international flair. The small size of the award-winning boutique firm ensures that homeowners receive highly personalized attention from start to finish, resulting in spaces that surpass expectations.

Left: The challenging spatial layout of the Upper East Side apartment didn't restrict creativity, but instead led to an adaptation of design tools to focus on intricate detail as well as rich material.
Photograph by Charlotte Hagen-Cazes

Left & Below: The design's material palette of stone, wood, and fabrics features fumed Acacia wood from Germany, Buxy stone from France, and silk and linens from India. Thoughtfully chosen lighting complements the space and highlights the custom details.

Facing Page: To elevate the apartment's existing architecture of long hallways, the transition from one room to another was designed to become a visual experience. Along these passages are carefully choreographed views of New York City. Materials, furniture placement, and color palettes were carefully selected to complement the view rather than to compete with it.

Photographs by Charlotte Hagen-Cazes

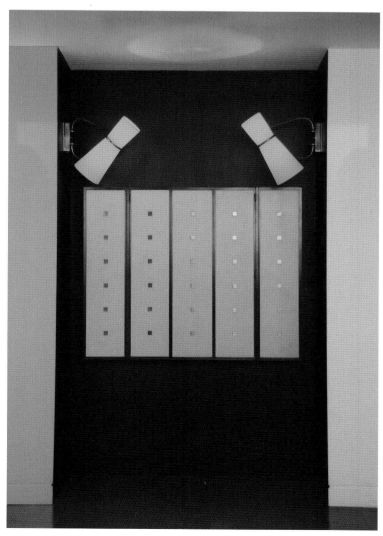

Above, Right & Facing Page: All custom-designed elements and details—media room with hidden TV lift, integrated lighting solutions, floor-to-ceiling pivot doors, custom built-ins with floating shelves, concealed hardware—were seamlessly and functionally integrated into the design. The artwork is carefully placed and balanced, resulting in a refined and elegant interior that is understated and highly livable.
Photographs by Charlotte Hagen-Cazes

et si
le rêve
était
réalité?

Posh Exclusive Interiors

New York

Monique Breaux, the founder of Posh Exclusive Interiors, is an agent of beauty and balance, carefully crafting spaces that are fit for exhibition. For over 20 years, Monique has used her talents to create thoughtful, vibrant interiors that dazzle the eye. From the great halls of grand estates to the trendy lofts of Manhattan's elite, Posh Exclusive Interiors promises an authentic artistic interpretation of the owner. When designing homes with a contemporary vibe, Monique combines simplicity and color to build rooms that are at once understated and full of expression. With passion and persistence, Monique has breathed life into countless interiors, challenging herself at every turn to create something individual and intellectual.

Left: A well-balanced foyer leads to a simple sitting room. In a contemporary setting, things can appear very sterile, so it is important to add foliage and flowers to express warmth in the space and reflect that the home is more than able to nurture life.
Photograph by Evan Jones

Above: The master bedroom is covered in shades of midnight, and with a skyline view of the city the pillowtop bedding practically floats into the night sky. The scarlet wall, art, and floral arrangement are rich, but not overbearing.
Photograph by Anastassio Mentis

Right: From the shower's clear doors, the owner can look out onto the city. The room features marble and is bathed in natural light, so everything seems natural and peaceful.
Photograph by Anastassio Mentis

Facing Page Top: The study is outfitted with an oversized sofa that converts to a guest bed. I custom-designed the surrounding chairs so that they enhanced comfort and didn't obstruct the gorgeous view of the city. The featured painting is full of color to counter the slate and almond shades in the home.
Photograph by Kim Sargent

Facing Page Bottom: Everything in the living room points to the sprawling windows, which give way to a beautiful view. Color patterns are repeated in the flowers and painting, as well as the midnight-blue chairs and the adjacent bedroom. The sectional makes a perfect reading nook.
Photograph by Kim Sargent

Sagart Studio

Washington, D.C.

The complexity of European minimalistic sensibilities and the adventuresome spirit of the American homeowner define the portfolio of Vincent Sagart. When taking on a home—whether in D.C., the West Coast, or overseas—Vincent transforms rooms into spaces where everyday life and elegance meet one another, even in the smallest details. The primary elements of wood, stone, and light frequently come together to create a cohesive space, and whenever possible, design ideas are rooted in the local landscape. In 1999, Vincent and his wife Helena, an artist in her own right, launched their full-service design studio in Washington, D.C., amid neighborhoods filled with beautiful historic homes. Their showroom represents exclusive European manufacturers of kitchens, dressing rooms, cabinetry, lighting, and bath products. In addition to his design work, Vincent shares his passion as an adjunct professor at Marymount University. His work has been featured on HGTV and in countless international publications.

Left: The modern kitchen is a wonderful example of a harmonious blending of materials and surfaces that make their own statement. Complete with sophisticated Kreon lighting, the cozy indoor space is sculpted so that it is visually connected to the home's exterior. This attention to detail and reverence for design helps to blend the façade of the historic D.C. home with its contemporary heart.
Photograph by Sagart Studio

Above & Facing Page Left: A place for rest and relaxation, the master bedroom suite features a dark, peaceful color palette. The dark tones give way to lighter hues as the homeowner travels from the bedroom to the bath. Custom-designed Poliform wardrobes and vanity were seamlessly integrated into the interior architecture of the master bedroom. Each space flows into the next with no physical or visual interruption.

Facing Page Right: Only the most essential elements are included in the kitchen. Although it is a space that is small in size, it benefits from clean lines of warm wood cabinets and a flowing design plan. A place for the family to gather, the kitchen features an indoor grill and powerful canopy hood. It is truly a chef's kitchen.

Photographs by Sagart Studio

"The best spaces give the homeowner everyday luxury and elegance."
Vincent Sagart

"Honoring the architectural materials of the house is essential in design."
Vincent Sagart

Above Left: The Zen-like bathroom was reduced to the primary materials of water, light, and stone. The custom washbasin pairs seamlessly with the rest of the grey and white elements in the austere space. Basking in a flood of soothing natural light, the bathtub—set in a slab of pure white stone—is surrounded by rough-surfaced grey tile.

Above Right: The historic Capitol Hill townhouse brings together European sensibilities while paying homage to something that's very American: a diversity of cultures. Editing the space through every stage of the renovation allowed us to feature the brick wall as a part of the space, while paring down the furniture, art, and accessories allows individual elements to come together to tell a story.

Facing Page Right: With a reverence toward irregularity, roughness, and bareness, the kitchen serves as design inspiration. The brick wall is complemented beautifully with richly textured and colored mahogany flooring. Its imperfections only add to the uniqueness of the space. White painted brushed pine cabinetry plays against the honed limestone countertops with hundreds of tiny, petrified fossils.
Photographs by Sagart Studio

Studio Santalla

Washington, D.C.

Ernesto Santalla is an architect, but he is very interested in the purity of the interior. With knowledge and experience in every facet of the industry, from picking out art to complex structural issues, he is able to advise on all angles of the design process. He designs rooms that are both efficient and visually stunning, a combination that defines understated elegance. Ensuring that every element in the room has a purpose allows Ernesto to create spaces that focus on quality over quantity. He designs with a belief that luxury isn't defined by opulence and excess, but instead by the merit and durability of products. The resulting spaces are long-lasting testaments to the balance of form and function.

Left: Everything in a house has its own character, but there is a common thread that runs throughout, tying all the elements together. In a small space, it was important to efficiently maximize all the available square footage. By hiding the wires for the AV equipment, for instance, the room appears clean, well-edited, and perfectly balanced.
Photograph by Alan Karchmer

"Seamless integration is about developing spaces in which everything has a specific place or purpose—creating a beautiful room with no obvious intervention."

Ernesto Santalla

Above: Three main areas are integrated within one large open space: working, seating, and sleeping. The sleep area is positioned behind a low wall, which is a permanent element used to subtly define the room. Decorative elements also delineate space, such as an expansive area rug that defines the main seating area. Special care was taken to ensure sprinkler heads, audio-visual and electrical wiring, and switching were invisible, creating a flawless environment.

Facing Page Left: Function and aesthetics unite in the home's workspace. A large-scale sculpture by Nelson Carrilho is set on a pedestal, which is integrated into the custom-designed, space-defining desk.

Facing Page Right: Contrasts of industrial and modern design and smooth versus rough fill the space and color acts as the unifying element. The loft's structural elements are left exposed and the new construction is inserted within the context.

Photographs by Geoffrey Hodgdon

Above: Old is new again in a former dining space, now used as an indoor seating area. The focus is on the fireplace, which was rebuilt to harmonize with the architecture of the space.

Right: A library, the point of entry from a courtyard, provides a comfortable retreat within the home. Integrating new construction with an ancient building required structural considerations, such as adding a concrete beam to support the floor above.

Facing Page Top: The only addition to the existing structure, a new kitchen is positioned on the top level of an ancient home in the town of Rasteau, France. The fully functional, contemporary design is open to the gorgeous view and the adjacent terrace.

Facing Page Bottom: A perfectly preserved ceiling—the architectural statement of the space—illustrates the traditional architecture of Provence. The oddly shaped room, built in another era, was reworked to suit modern needs.
Photographs by Geoffrey Hodgdon

"A tight budget is no excuse for poor design."
Ernesto Santalla

Above: The in-law quarters are distinct and separate from the main home, yet the contemporary style is still complementary to the home's traditional style. Crisp, white furnishings contribute to the overall fresh, bright design.

Facing Page: A contemporary pub within an inn makes a high impact statement. The design aims to take the rustic nature of a traditional "country" inn theme and replace it with bursts of modernity.
Photographs by Geoffrey Hodgdon

Design Specifications, page 235

Billy Blanco Designs, page 297

Pepe Calderin Design, page 351

Collins & Dupont Interior Design, page 321

southeast

Design Specifications

Florida

Navigating the design process can be difficult for homeowners, but according to Wendy Kensler's philosophy, the process should be fun and relaxing. Working with builders, architects, and owners from the ground up, Wendy and the rest of the team at Design Specifications provide indoor and outdoor space planning and design, as well as full project management. With an attention to detail and homeowners' needs, Wendy creates spaces specific to the lifestyles of the people who occupy them. From very formal, traditional spaces to sleek contemporary homes, Design Specifications stands ready to make owners' visions become reality. But it's more than that; Wendy's goal is to make sure owners wake up every morning, in love with their home.

Left: Rustic, family-friendly, and welcoming, the living room and kitchen exude an Old World charm. Hand-shaped and hand-glazed tile adorns the backsplash in the kitchen, and the space is all about the rustic stone, brick, and wood elements. Appliances are concealed and the cabinetry is back-lit for a subtle effect.
Photograph courtesy of Everett and Soule

"Consider how the room will be used before deciding anything else."
Wendy Kensler

Above: Antique terracotta mosaic tile in the foyer is complemented by the oversized arched walnut doors of seeded glass and ribbons of hand twisted wrought iron. Behind the entry table, an antique mirror wall with a subtle harlequin pattern reflects natural light through the space.

Facing Page: The dining room is the most formal spot in the house. The walls and ceiling are faux painted with a blue Venetian plaster. The wrought iron and rock crystal chandelier and sconces create the ambiance for a romantic and elegant candlelit dinner.
Photographs courtesy of Everett and Soule

Above: Shades of red and chocolate brown velvet make the master bedroom a romantic Old World-inspired retreat. Walnut is used throughout the sitting room to match the reclaimed walnut floors. Gold leaf in the center of the ceiling accents the architectural details of the space.

Facing Page: The gallery stretches from the family room to the master bedroom on the lake side of the house. The multiple colored cut crystal and wrought iron chandeliers are reminiscent of ancient cathedrals. In the arches, the bricks were intentionally left exposed to reinforce the Old World theme.

Photographs courtesy of Everett and Soule

"Every detail should make the homeowner happy."
Wendy Kensler

"Even a modest initial idea can develop into a reality that surpasses all expectation."
Wendy Kensler

Left: The lowest floor of a Florida home opens out to an impressive pool. Originally a simple room with textured walls, the brick and wood ceiling and stone walls were installed during the renovation, transforming the space completely. Built-in wine shelving and carved panels distinguish the cabinetry, making the space feel like it's in the center of California wine country. Oversized nail head trim on the chairs and the plank top table give guests a luxurious space to gather during wine events and dinner parties.
Photograph courtesy of Everett and Soule

Interiors by JSD Corporation

Florida

Noreen Sachs romances rooms on paper; Jeffrey makes sure the angles work out. She's quite adept at renderings; he has an encyclopedic, hands-on knowledge of milling, finishing, and scale. Together they form the multifaceted brain trust behind Interiors by JSD Corporation, a full-service design house specializing in transforming dirt lots into dramatic showpieces and tired pied-à-terres into splendid retreats. By bringing together their skills in furniture design, architectural layout, scale, proportion, and history, there is very little this duo cannot accomplish. Together they transform homes, yachts, and offices into livable spaces that are touted worldwide.

Left: Going from an initial concept to completion in the Breakers West Country Club in West Palm Beach, we were able to create a home that the whole family could grow into. Sink bases for the master bath were crafted from purchased Habersham cabinetry, centered by a custom, matching lower vanity topped in a bow-front, ogee-edged, Emperador Brown marble top. With an open space plan, the mirrors, tub, and two sided, walk-in Roman shower remain fully accessible. By selecting and designing all the materials and patterns, from moulding and mosaic inlays to Damask handpainted wallcoverings, we created a visually extraordinary and functional master bath. Balancing light with dimmable wall sconces, chandeliers, and recessed lighting, the homeowner can achieve the maximum effect for both daytime and evening.
Photograph by Joseph Stern

Above: For a powder room like no other, we treated the walls with a striking, lacquered, espresso-brown craft-paper wallcovering with a watermarked finish from Maya Romanoff. The groin ceiling we designed was handpainted in a contrasting faux finish to echo the design of the chandelier, complementing the ornate bronze mirror over a carved wood chest that was transformed into an exquisite vanity. Marble wainscoting travels halfway up the walls with black marble mosaic set beneath a carved stone border. The dramatic formal features of the space are reminiscent of the formulas for scale and proportion established by Greek and Roman architecture.

Facing Page: The living room is the hub of the residence, open to an arched loft area and with a curved wood and iron staircase. By designing and fabricating all aspects of the room—from the antiqued, glazed fireplace and antiqued, mirrored trumeau above to the faux wood-like ceiling beams and 21-inch-high crown moulding—we were able to craft a very exact ambience. The golden painted walls, stone floor, and floor-to-ceiling front and back bar set the tone for function as well as a grand space. The bar's Rainforest stone top has a sandblasted top, which is reminiscent of old European castles. The handpainted candelabra chandelier further accentuates the scale and proportion of the room, while Moroccan-like sconces on either side of the fireplace and persimmon sheers flanked by solid-colored side panels and silk plaid fabric valances help create the atmosphere.

Photographs by Joseph Stern

"Architecture and interior design are inextricably, beautifully linked."
Jeffrey Bellfy

Above: The homeowner desired a library with rich woods, leading us to design and fabricate solid raised-panel cherry walls and ceiling beams encased with cherry crown. Double doors and pocket doors leading into the room were faux-finished to match. Functional and warm, inviting and inspirational, the cozy workplace is a surprising retreat.

Facing Page: Stepping down into the wine cellar from the living room is like being transported into another world. A herringbone brick floor and 15-inch-thick entryway, along with the iron arched entry gates, make the most of authentic materials, while custom-designed wine storage and a tall wine cooler encased in the same wood finish brings everything into the present. A handpainted red corking station and original canvas ceiling mural we painted—representing long life, fertility, truth and knowledge, and prosperity—make the charming space inviting and luxurious from all six dimensions. The room is the homeowners' favorite escape from everyday activities.
Photographs by Joseph Stern

Left: A faux-wood-beamed, coffered ceiling in the kitchen and raised-panel, glass-front upper cabinet doors with glass backs naturally illuminated an otherwise solid wall of cabinetry. Custom-finished appliqués from Decorators Supply installed on the hood complement the perimeter cabinetry. Two large islands, the second set on an angle, feature pivoting, caned-back chairs that can face either the kitchen or the great room and playroom beyond. The mixture of wood, glass, and granite set against a marble floor maximizes casual family living. An archway leads into the butler's pantry, enhanced by metal and glass hanging lanterns by Currey and Company.
Photograph by Joseph Stern

J. Edwards Interiors

Alabama

Jenny Edwards designs homes that are purely an expression of each inhabitant, using fabrics, furniture, flooring, and accessories that complement the homeowners' personal style. Her designs promote classic lines and neutral tones highlighted with bursts of color, with her eye for space planning allowing Jenny to create functional spaces that boast flow and creativity. By enhancing the architectural elements of a space, her layouts work in tandem with the environment, sometimes even using the outdoor landscape to complement the interior design. Each of her layouts boasts personality, style, and, most importantly, a timeless design to last the life of the home.

Left: When designing the living area, I focused on its strong architectural setting. The woods beyond the windows provided great inspiration, so I kept the interior very natural and neutral, adding pops of color and a few feature pieces here and there. The tapestry serves as a beautiful focal point and also balances the fireplace on the opposite wall. An iron chandelier with painted gold accents helps the space be the perfect mix of dressy and casual.
Photograph by Brian Francis

Above Left & Right: As the entrance point, the foyer sets the tone of the home. Framed prints and the unique wrought iron table create up-to-date traditional style. In the living room, classic elements give the room an air of sophistication, such as the antique clock paired with the traditional grand piano. Light and airy fabrics offset the heaviness of the piano, making the space airy and inviting.

Right: The bedroom continues the home's color palette, picking up the creams, greens, and blues. These soft colors provide a calming ambience, perfect for a peaceful night's rest.

Facing Page: I wanted the dining room and open kitchen to feel very comfortable, a place where the homeowners could sit and relax with a cup of coffee while reading the newspaper. It is a gathering space, and the slipcovered leathers chairs near the fireplace further promote the room's welcoming ambience.
Photographs by Brian Francis

Jacquelyn Narrell
Architectural Interior Design

Texas

Jacquelyn Narrell has never been more passionate in her genuine pursuit of design excellence, impeccably tailoring living environments around the world. Certified in architectural interior design in Chelsea, London, in 1994, she melds her knowledge and international experience to develop unparalleled, distinctive living spaces. With this philosophy and her effervescent *joie de vivre*, she balances inspiration and commitment imbued with architectural integrity, beautiful aesthetic, and clever functionality. Confident in her vast library of global resources, Jacque's profound dedication and referral of her life's work remains key to her personal and professional foundational success. Based in the Dallas area, her eponymous firm serves an elite clientele throughout the United States, including Hawaii and Alaska, and abroad.

Left: Inspired by travels throughout Europe, France, Italy, and the spectacular coastlines of Sicily, the luxurious Roman bath boasts a decadent spa nestled within the interior walls of its majestic brick fortress. Elegant soothing water features add ornamental detail to an atmosphere of serene tranquility. Planters and pots found in Rome, softly sculpted with lifelike facial features, exude personality and spirit. Lush, elevated manicured gardens silhouette a façade of intimate privacy as stunning views lend vibrant architectural history. A winding path leading to the magnificent flagstone staircase vividly enhances the master plan's attention to finite detail of the rocky yet formal landscape. A maze sprinkled high above the courtyard makes the perfect setting where magical tea parties come to life.
Photograph by Dan Piassick Photography

"Designing is what I do. It's my passion, my heart, and soul embedded deep in my DNA. Anyone who knows me knows this is who I am. I can never deny it." *Jacque Dunbar Narrell*

Left: Old World charm divinely defines an elaborate outdoor oasis. Comfortable surroundings lure dedicated sun worshipers to revel in the highest level of relaxation. Fragrant flowers provide a verdant respite inside perennial English walled gardens. Sprigs of blooming color gleam brightly over the elusive enclosure, while plantings on the ivy-covered stone wall showcase the formal sanctuary. A trickling water fountain towers brilliantly, adding unique dimension and sound to an unforgettable vintage scheme. An alfresco patio bursting with Mediterranean indulgence provides poolside dining at its best. The dinette-bench ensemble, composed of finely ground marble and sandstone, was made exclusively in Naples to add the perfect finishing touch.
Photograph by Dan Piassick Photography

Above Left: Tip a hat Southern-style as spun driftwood stools belly up to the fully stocked bar in customary Wild West saloon tradition. Chiseled hollow columns reminiscent of waterfalls built around San Antonio's River Walk were purchased in The Stockyards of local Fort Worth. Filled onsite of liquid concrete, the columns were positioned under the restored staircase and trimmed out on the original brick floors, adding historical flair to a Texas oil man's family retreat.

Above Right: Boutique-style wine racks toasting the property's fruitful acreage line cellar walls behind a forged wrought iron door from Mexico. Upholstered, bullion-fringed slipper chairs positioned on scraped oak strip floors summon guests for decadent wine tastings. A customized island cabinet on casters, practical for serving, lends freedom to the space. Adjustable tavern sconce lighting shadows the natural wood trim and beams, giving ambience to the open cellar.

Facing Page: A bronze buffalo reigns supreme as bountiful furnishings grace the Dallas ranch's main house dining room. Amassed in grand stature, the spectacular home sets apart casual elegance for "grandeur entertaining." The Remington *Cattle Drive* takes center stage, surrounded by extensive refurbishments and commissioned cowboy art by Texas artist Mark McCord that pays homage to a bygone era. The Maitland Smith antler chandelier from Scotland accentuates King Ranch Axis deer hide seating, amidst turquoise-embellished décor.
Photographs by Dan Piassick Photography

"The moment every door bursts open, you want to hear, 'Wow!'"
Jacque Dunbar Narrell

"Our home is a tapestry of life, love, and the essence of our growing family. But most of all, what memories are made of."
Jacque Dunbar Narrell

Above: Designed exclusively for our beautiful granddolls, my innate concept and imagery was meant to forever inspire their creativity. Lovingly dubbed "The Granddolls' Parlour," generations of dolls, prized heirlooms, portraits, and books expand vivid imagination in the cheerfully painted fairytale wonderland of make-believe. Sunlight peeking through tiny shutters over a cozy window seat illuminates sweeping hues of soft rainbow pastels creating fantasy, befitting royalty. Artist Mark McCord paints billowy clouds across imaginary skies over Paris, summoning Tour Eiffel as winds whip gently through a colorfully striped circus tent. A petite Victorian suite was high bid at auction at the Louisiana Governor's Mansion. I spotted the flowery carpet in the antique district on Champs-Elysees, deep in the heart of Paris. Beyond a hidden doorway is a stuffed, miniature tea room. When our splendid new "grande-sons" join the party, their liveliness gives bold meaning to the phrase "bulls in a china shop." My grandchildren remain my greatest joy, my legacy.

Facing Page: The manor home's decidedly British formal dining hall, filled with European furnishings, embodies an unpretentious yet truly exquisite presence. A Regency buffed-mahogany, pie crust-edge dining table rests on double baluster-turned shafts with splayed scroll legs. A set of 12 George III dining chairs, covered in Gainsborough silk damask seating, boast cabriole legs with claw and ball feet. A bust of Eugenia of Versailles, festively masked for Carnivale, sits on a William IV pedestal. Chinese porcelain, a gift from my husband, graces the Georgian fireplace mantel found on Portobello Road in London. A fine-cut Venetian mirror rescued from a demolished French château reflects the regal Waterford chandelier and candelabras. A classic Edwardian tallboy with pediment cornice flanks the lavish window. Embroidered tapestry and Austrian blinds were rolled up in a suitcase on a girls' trip from Venice. I designed the beveled glass china showcase in-studio at my shop on Putney High Street in London.
Photographs by Dan Piassick Photography

Patricia McLean Interiors

Georgia

Considered a true, traditional designer, Patricia McLean, who founded her interior design business in 1985, specializes in the customization of paint colors, finishes, and fabrics, and layering of antiques and accessories. Guiding homeowners through construction to ensure the architectural bones are correct for furniture placement and flow is paramount to Patricia's design philosophy. A graduate of The University of Georgia with a bachelor's degree in furnishings and interiors, Patricia was selected to restore the ballroom in The Governor's Mansion and has been featured in many show houses. The Atlanta Symphony Associates Decorators' Show House earned her the ASID Design Excellence Award for The St. Regis Atlanta. She also received The Institute of Classical Architecture's Philip Shutze Residential Interior Design Award and The University of Georgia Bulldog 100. Her firm takes an organic approach to the design process, bringing Patricia's refined taste, fresh approach, vast resources, and *joie de vivre* to each project.

Left: I was hired by The St. Regis Hotel Residences to design a 4,000-square-foot model home in the hotel's high-rise condominiums. My firm was given carte blanche and we designed every aspect of the layout, from the floorplans and renderings to the custom furniture, art, antiques, upholstery, drapery, carpet, lighting, accessories, paint colors, bedding, and floor materials. Color plays a large role in the condo's overall design, especially in the entrance hall. I hand-mixed the terracotta-toned paint, which contrasts vividly against the crisp white architectural millwork. The eight-panel Chinoiserie screen was mounted to accentuate the panels. A Regency-inspired bench is covered in a sumptuous Italian textile featuring an ikat pattern that inspired the home's color palette. The pattern and palette of the marble floors were designed for a high-impact entry.
Photograph by Brian Gassel

"I love to combine English, French, and Italian furniture and antiques with Chinoiserie accents for an established look." *Patricia McLean*

Above: The living room's Oushak-style rug establishes the traditional color palette for the room. One of the specifications from the St. Regis Residences was to incorporate a 60-inch television. To meet this challenge, I custom designed the stately breakfront with English grillwork in the side doors and flamed mahogany center section, concealing the flatscreen. An antique telescope peers out from the window, framed by the luxurious silk draperies on gilt rods.

Facing Page Top: The dining room is defined by a collection of hand-painted Chinoiserie panels framed in bamboo. An ornate English mirror over the sideboard is balanced by antique alabaster lamps. A charming celadon-painted toile and crystal chandelier adds a touch of drama and crowns the room. The bespoke gilt window pelments with silk panels and silk loop trim address the single window and sliding balcony door with panache.

Facing Page Bottom: I mixed the wall color especially for the master bedroom and penned it "Patricia's Peach." At sunset, the color of the horizon becomes the same as the walls. The serpentine upholstered headboard adds elegance and allows homeowners to read comfortably in bed. The hand-woven crewel fabric is paired with green silk that matches the foliage in the Tree of Life design. The peach velvet bench speaks to the warm wall tone, while a pair of antique French chairs flanks the window niche. Small footstools were custom designed with bullion fringe to fit the chairs. An antique Italian gilt chandelier adds a final touch of luxury to the refined space.
Photographs by Brian Gassel

B Pila Design Studio

Florida

For Bea Pila-Gonzalez, principal designer and owner of B Pila Design Studio, design begins with a space's form. Passionate about architecture, Bea often looks at the shape of a piece of furniture and how it will integrate into the space before she begins to consider the material it will be made from. For Bea, it's second nature to start with space planning. The flow of a room is integral for any design, whether it is in the renovation of a luxury apartment or a build that she works on from the ground up. She not only loves design, she loves people. One of Bea's greatest joys is to bring the ideas of homeowners to life. Her portfolio of work represents this value. Her spaces, which integrate personal art collections and almost always include custom millwork, are as individual and varied as the people who occupy them. This is what brings homeowners back to B Pila Design Studio time after time.

Left: Balinese influences are seen throughout the contemporary vacation home located on ocean-front property in Key Biscayne. I selected an oversized aqua green sectional that mimics the color of the ocean just beyond the panoramic windows. The adjacent kitchen and breakfast nook benefit from the open floor plan that allows for easy movement and views of the ocean. Beautiful white paint accentuates the dark-toned woods and embedded pockets allow the draperies to completely recess into the ceiling for uninterrupted views. My favorite piece in the room is the oversized coffee table made from wood planks and a steel base. It is reminiscent of distressed Key West siding and completely child-proof.
Photograph by Robin Hill

"Design is a necessity, not a luxury." *Bea Pila-Gonzalez*

Above: Although the kitchen was part of a renovation, the space had to be completely redone. The previous kitchen was on the second floor, so it was brought downstairs and we built a completely new space. The Asian-inspired redesign gave the modern-contemporary home the warm up the homeowners desired. Beautiful Brazilian walnut and teak woods were introduced into the space and the curved border of the kitchen floor was made possible by the use of poured terrazzo. The effect is a luminous one and contrasts boldly with the wood grain in the walnut floors and teak cabinetry. The glass mosaic backsplash provides a backdrop for the asymmetrical stainless steel hood that was made especially for the space. Bamboo fibers are embedded into the floating countertop that serves double duty as a bar. The eat-in bench adjacent to the island is perfect for casual dining and the curved lines in the floor and ceiling serve to distinguish the rooms without the use of walls.
Photograph by Manuel Buzengo

Facing Page: In the outdoor living room, the landscape provides the walls. Curtains provide protection from the elements, while the fully functional fireplace makes for a romantic focal point. I always try to design outdoor living spaces as I would indoor rooms. Seating arrangements should never be created with matched pieces of furniture. To accentuate the stunning ceiling, custom lighting was installed to light the space in the shape of a square, giving it the drama it deserves.
Photograph by Lapeyra Photography

"Ideas are the most valuable tool we have."
Bea Pila-Gonzalez

Top and Middle: He was a classicist and she was a modernist, so I had to bring the two styles together in the Key Biscayne home seamlessly. The living room features an elongated coffered ceiling and stunning views of the ocean. Transitional furnishings pair beautifully with the large-scale modern painting hung above the sofa. In the library, as well as the living room, I worked with the architect from the home's conception to design the millwork and trey ceiling in the impressive and masculine space.
Photographs by Lapeyra Photography

Bottom: In a French-inspired home, the owner wanted a bedroom that featured shades of blue and soft green. The sleigh bed is flanked by Hollywood Regency-style mirrored nightstands. Many of the room's accessories—from the mirror's frame to the bedside lamps—feature mother of pearl accents. The ceiling peaks in an oval above the bed, adding a touch of romance to the elegant space.
Photograph by George Cott

Facing Page Top: Although the kitchen may look simple and streamlined, the look wasn't achieved without a significant amount of work. Absolutely everything was designed to fit perfectly into the space. The massive mahogany island contains two refrigerated drawers, a dishwasher, and other hidden appliances. Its marble top had to be specially ordered and carefully seamed to provide a polished work surface. An antique dinner table with a diameter of 72 inches sits in the breakfast nook next to a built-in buffet. As with most of my designs, I worked directly with the architect in the design phase of the house to craft all of the millwork for the kitchen. The painted cabinets match the rest of the millwork in the home and the mushroom-colored chairs offer a hint of casual elegance to the space.
Photograph by Carlos Domenech

Facing Page Bottom: The Key Biscayne apartment was once two residences, which gives the combined space a total of 7,000 square feet. The homeowners were collectors of glass pieces, so I had to work them into the space. A Chihuly chandelier makes for a breathtaking focal point in the great room, positioned next to the large windows that look out onto the ocean. Art Deco pieces—some antique and others imported from modern Italian designers—serve as seating and serving surfaces. In the foyer, a curvilinear soffit winds around the space to create a wavelike movement. A large nautilus shell design is embedded into the floor just inside the front door. The lighting cove in the center of the space directs the eye toward the center of the room. Set on an angle, the huge space possesses a unique feeling of movement that draws one's attention toward the glass sculptures, Warhol collection, and the ocean beyond.
Photograph by John Gillan

Beasley & Henley
Interior Design

Florida

Whether it's old Hollywood glamour, Las Vegas showmanship, or the natural marshlands of the Atlantic coast, Troy Beasley is inspired by anything "out of the box." Troy and his partner Stephanie Henley—who plays with numbers so he can play with designs—founded Beasley & Henley Interior Design in 1993. Since that time, Troy and Stephanie have become mainstays in Florida design, creating luxurious spaces for homeowners and contributing to various national and regional design publications as expert columnists. The boutique firm specializes in concepts from simple and sleek spaces in natural tones to over-the-top gathering rooms inspired by the Rat Pack's stomping grounds. Regardless of a room's design, fluidity and effortless comfort are the ultimate goals for Troy, but when he teams up with a homeowner, very little is simply left to chance.

Left: I like creating a fluid space with curves and lots of interesting pieces to enjoy. The curves, including those in the ceiling, keep the eye moving about the room. Some of the interesting pieces include the mid-century chairs close to the window, which join custom-designed, organically shaped "tree trunk" coffee tables. The tile on the wall behind the television creates interest because it is material typically reserved for flooring. The randomness of the rug's design is fun and a bit whimsical, but the main focus of the room is the marshland outside, which was the driving force behind the design. I wanted to relate the interior curves to the exterior waves of the water.
Photograph by Stephen Allen

Above: The dark crossbeam ceiling against white walls creates a truly stand-out effect. A neutral palette establishes a cozy ambience immediately upon entering the room, and pops of blue in throw pillows and chairs add a splash of color.

Facing Page: The Las Vegas-inspired dining room is all about height and drama. The two-story room is anchored by the heavy, though relatively simple, fireplace that rises behind the Versace dining table and dramatic seating. The chandeliers are lit by LEDs and change color with a flip of a switch. They are floating sculptures.
Photographs by Stephen Allen

"You need something in the space that adds tension to keep it interesting and the eye moving." *Troy Beasley*

"The best design inspiration comes from reaching outside your comfort zone."
Stephanie Henley

Top: Glitzy mirrored nightstands cozy up to the back wall of the bedroom, which serves as the headboard for the bed. Its chocolate brown squares create a textural balance with the shiny and smooth qualities of the accent furniture. The flat dome in the ceiling is adorned in silver leaf to mimic the nightstands, while the square of the ceiling reflects the pattern in the headboard.

Bottom: I designed the partners' desk specifically for the office space. Its modern construction is balanced by the antique reproduction chest against the wall. Huge horizontal stripes over-accentuate the space, and the unexpected antler chandelier gives the room something unique.

Facing Page Top: The big salon space—perfect for entertaining—was designed with a lounge concept in mind. The large bar is textured with mini red mosaic tiles; the glass shelves beyond it appear to be floating in golden space. The round rug and four circular gold leaf domes in the ceiling play off each other in this great mix of traditional design and contemporary tone.

Facing Page Bottom: Influenced by Hollywood glam, the daughter's suite utilizes various bright pinks against a black and white palette. Marilyn Monroe's likeness graces the traditional chairs, which face the modern sofa in the sitting area. Iconic order columns fuse with the playful pinks in the space, and the thick rug atop the wood plank floors keeps the sitting area comfortable and welcoming.
Photographs by Stephen Allen

Brinson Interiors

Alabama

Wayne Brinson Holder has always had an eye for the finer things, so stepping into the design field was a fitting move. Even as a child, he gravitated to the arts, appreciating everything from porcelain and paintings to floral design and antiques. This respect for refinement allows Wayne to saturate a project with fine furnishings, resplendent color palettes, and a precise application of scale and proportion. He begins cultivating an idea for each design by choosing a particular piece, such as a painting, and builds the design around it. With this skill, he has the ability to create designs in any style, from a rustic hunting lodge to an opulent private estate.

Left: The seeds of inspiration for the large den area sprouted from both family tradition and the homeowner's appreciation of exquisite furnishings. They hail from a long line of hunters, so the space pays homage to the sport, using edgy color and pattern choices highlighted by rich gold finishes. The large art piece, which hangs above a hand-disstressed leather sofa, came from the family's hunting camp. A Lucite coffee table paired with a zebra print armchair is a perfect example of the room's visual contrast. Each element in the design, such as the armoire and lush Oriental rug, was chosen with careful consideration. From construction to finalized design, the home took a full 17 years to complete.
Photograph by Miller Mobley

Above: By sticking to authentic pieces, both period contemporary and period antique can easily coexist. In the living room, the combination of period antiques, such as a French settee, crystal chandelier, and marble and gilt candelabras, are paired with updated upholstery and contemporary art.

Left: A free-floating curved staircase adds a sophisticated architectural element to the foyer, highlighted by a leopard print stair runner. To personalize the space, the homeowner's collection of art is displayed on facing foyer walls.

Facing Page: When a design achieves a sense of balance, it gives the mind the perception of serenity. A combination of organic and antiqued elements delivers a stunning arrangement in the foyer. Atop the antique French chest sits a natural piece of ivory cup coral, which rests on a stainless steel base. A pair of antique French gilt chairs flank the coral, creating perfect symmetry.
Photographs by Miller Mobley

"My inspiration comes from individual objects rather than a particular style."
Wayne Brinson Holder

Above & Right: To create a tranquil retreat, the use of both larger pieces and smaller components make the space comfortable and plush. The faux-finished poster bed features a tester, draped in rich silks. Layer upon layer of creamy hues and soft textures create a reposeful environment, and details such as silk-embroidered pillows add little touches of luxury.

Facing Page Top: By introducing contemporary elements against more traditional design pieces, the dining room is lifted to a level of elegant sophistication. The antique Venetian mirror, which hangs above a period antique French enfilade, magnifies the room's reflective elements. An antique crystal and porcelain chandelier crowns the layout.

Facing Page Bottom: In the study, a bold mirrored fireplace wall adds depth to the space. An oversized ottoman plays with proportion while providing the homeowner with a spacious sitting area. A faux-finished tortoise and gold-leaf tray ceiling create a metallic element that pairs beautifully with the antique brass chandelier. The chandelier—the room's inspiration—once resided in a local historic hotel.
Photographs by Miller Mobley

C L Studio, Inc.

Florida

Coco Chanel recommended that ladies look in the mirror and take one thing off before leaving the house. Like the negative space of a painting or periods of silence in a symphony, Mlle. Chanel knew that simplicity was elegance in practice. In similar fashion, Jose J. Cabrera of C L Studio, Inc. embraces a philosophy of simplicity with refined ease as he collaborates with homeowners to create a space that surpasses their imagination. With a passion for the unexpected, Jose combines dynamic colors and designs with simple, clean lines to create a balance that is at once interesting and luxurious. By eliminating the frivolous aspects that can find their way into a design, Jose allows the necessary objects of a room to speak for themselves without cluttering the space with superfluous elements.

Left: The grand salon of our magnificent penthouse offers a million-dollar view of The City Beautiful. Within the dramatic floor-to-ceiling glass walls I combined a modern aesthetic with my signature cutting-edge style—the whole is indeed reflective of the sum of its parts. The unique juxtaposition of fine objects seamlessly works together to complement the entire room, blurring the lines of furniture and sculpture. A bold color palette contrasted with warm neutral tones serves to stimulate the senses.
Photograph by Uneek Image

Above & Facing Page Top: We spearheaded the LEVEL Hope & Help Center Designer Showcase 2011, benefiting the Hope & Help Center of Central Florida in its efforts to treat and prevent the spread of HIV/AIDS. The event presented us with the opportunity to create a living space full of energy and vibrant color. Natural wood grain seating and an organic side table sit near chrome chairs designed by Sami Hayek. Geometric patterns play in accent furniture and upon the custom Kyle Bunting rug.

Facing Page Bottom: Bold splashes of turquoise and coral against the neutral color palette add complexity to the room, which overlooks Lake Eola in downtown Orlando. I designed the lacquer turquoise console table for the space; the organic rock crystal drawer pulls are an unexpected accent that summarizes how I designed the space—juxtaposing the natural world with modern aesthetics. The two seating areas communicate well while remaining separate from one another.
Photographs by Uneek Image

Above: The mix of hard and smooth pieces with luxurious, soft surfaces is really sexy. In the home of Ike Taylor, a defensive back for the Pittsburgh Steelers, I integrated this concept of mixed textures and styles to create a home that is both welcoming and masculine. We used a combination of amber and grey tones throughout while combining modern and organic elements. In the master sitting room, a sculptural petrified wood table sits next to a classical revival klismos chair. The mid-century feel of the sofa is juxtaposed with the abstract painting above.

Facing Page: Lighting and circular forms are center stage in the two-story, post-modern living room. The ebony-stained architectural wall provides sculptural interest while serving as a backdrop for the modern bench placed in front. Circular disc lights dangle from the ceiling; the shape is reflected in accent furniture and patterns in the rug. Tones of caramel and charcoal grey mixed with natural hues add a vibrancy that translates to a very masculine tone.

Photographs by Uneek Image

"Truly great design should create atmospheres that evoke a casual elegance with a modern sensibility, both classic and timeless." *Jose J. Cabrera*

Above: Lake Butler—with relaxing hues and the reflections off the water—influenced the design, which includes azure blue, citron, and charcoal against a monochromatic background. With generous seating and a calming atmosphere, it is the perfect place for both entertaining and relaxing.
Photograph by Everett & Soulé

Facing Page: The master bathroom should be a retreat for the homeowners. Expansive, windowed doors open to a Zen garden, which may also be easily viewed from the wall of mirrors above the sinks. Onyx countertops and sleek cabinet faces create a spa-like feel. Horizontal stripes of alternating semi- and high-gloss paint in the same color adorn the wall beyond the bathtub; this is one of our signature design elements, and gently accents the neutral palette of the luxurious space.
Photographs by Stephen Allen Photography

Design Specifications

Florida

Unexpected design choices make for innovative homes. Such are the homes designed by Wendy Kensler, principal of Design Specifications. From outdoor poolside spaces to guest bedrooms every space is given the utmost attention to detail and consideration. Founded in 1987, Design Specifications specializes in innovative design solutions, and no idea is off-limits. Wendy has entertained suggestions for anything from rooftop mini-golf courses to an artificial cave complete with stalactites. While not all ideas are possible—a rooftop mini-golf course wasn't suitable for the neighborhood—Wendy does her best to accommodate every vision put forth by homeowners. The result is a reality that exceeds expectations. This, along with Wendy's engaging personality, brings owners back to Design Specifications time and again as their lifestyles and tastes evolve.

Left: Designed to entertain for intimate parties with a handful of friends or for elaborate charity events complete with a string quartet, the house exemplifies a playful elegance. Majestic columns feature panels of onyx that, when lit from within, absolutely glow. A huge grid of stone and wood gives the floor an unexpected linear quality while the Christopher Guy chairs in the corner draw the eye toward the tall windows and the view beyond.
Photograph courtesy of Everett and Soule

"No style is off limits; no idea is out of the question when designing the perfect environment."
Wendy Kensler

Above: The breakfast nook, family room, and bar come together in a cozy, welcoming space. The rectangular breakfast table seats eight, while the sofa provides seating for morning coffee. A sectional sits back-to-back with the sofa, which faces the rectilinear fireplace and provides a view of the kitchen.

Facing Page: The homeowners wanted the bar to be a focal complement to the amazing lake views on the other side of the lake. With room for two bartenders, the bar has ample size and is also a perfect serving area for family brunches. At night, the area is lit by three different kinds of lights: fiber optic, LED, and soft incandescent. It's the perfect place for parties any time of day.
Photographs courtesy of Everett and Soule

Above: Eight chaises, two sectionals and two pool beds encircle the symmetrical central pool. With plenty of seating at the dining tables both under the covered patio and at strategic points around the pool, it is the perfect backyard oasis for parties. Many of the design choices are an interpretation of an exotic resort pool the homeowners fell in love with while on vacation.

Left: Instead of a pair of chairs in the master bedroom's sitting area, a swing made from an antique Indian ox cart hangs from the ceiling with luxurious silk and velvet pillows. A relaxing place to watch the lake outside, the swing is a favorite among guests and partygoers who are drawn to its exotic-like appeal.

Facing Page: The outdoor kitchen provides opportunity to cook great food in a huge area for food preparation. Complete with a stainless steel grill and hood, the kitchen is adjacent to the music room, which may be separated from the space by glass corner doors. The stage, dance floor and sound-proof drapery of the music room allows for family jam sessions and professional musicians to enjoy the space.
Photographs courtesy of Everett and Soule

Above: The owners wanted each of their guest bedrooms to be different and utterly unique so that they could decide where to put each person, depending on their individual tastes. The Versailles Bedroom, alternatively referred to as the Marilyn Monroe Bedroom, is the epitome of elegance. The plush white carpet, mirrored four poster bed, and silver leaf on the ceiling come together to create a space that appeals to women and men alike. Colors of white, cream, and chocolate brown create a soothing palette while the damask wall covering—made with thousands of tiny glass beads—reflects light elegantly.

Facing Page: The upstairs wine room is a fun mix of elegance and playfulness. The climate-controlled section at the back of the room is divided from the rest of the space by crystal-clear glass. The natural wood slab table was cut so that it could continue on into this part of the room almost without interruption. Every chair is different and the floor is composed of various materials, from slate slabs to antique terracotta tiles and more.

Photographs courtesy of Everett and Soule

"Dress a space based on its function and the feelings you want it to evoke." *Wendy Kensler*

Interiors by JSD Corporation

Florida

Husband and wife duo Jeffrey Bellfy and Noreen Sachs share a rare symbiosis: thanks to his knowledge of furniture history, scale, and proportion, and her skill in creating renderings that are as artistic as they are inspired, the two have built a design empire that is more than the sum of its parts. Jeffrey approached interiors from the architectural end, working for Pierson Interiors in high school and learning furniture, construction, and finishing on the plant floor. Noreen studied art and design at the University of Michigan's School of Art & Architecture, emerging with a degree in interior design and ceramics, which she applies every day. Together they create highly customized transitional, traditional, and contemporary spaces that always feel fresh and innovative.

Left: In order to highlight the homeowners' love of African and Asian culture, we transformed a traditional home into an Asian-inspired contemporary space, mixing luxurious silk and velvet fabrics with textures and finishes to create a very specific ambience. In the master bedroom, we chose a lacquered Swaim bed with antique gold accents, custom built two night tables with glass tops—accentuated with John Richard Asian rectangular shaded lamps—and complemented it all with a forged-iron and wood bench from Tomlinson covered in a velvet cushion and hinged chenille bolsters.
Photograph by Joseph Stern

Above: The deep red powder room embodies an Asian influence, decorated with traditional Chinese ornaments such as gold lion head door knockers. A basin sink shines on top of the detailed, dark mahogany cabinet, adding a touch of glimmer to the room.

Facing Page: In the dining room, a persimmon wall glaze filled in and enhanced the former knockdown wall texture. We created the custom walnut dining table with ebony inlay and a reverse beveled edge in our own mill shop, and paired it with chairs in a gauffraged, kid-glove leather from Swaim. Throughout the room, hardware, appliqués, and textured glass continues the Asian influence.
Photograph by Joseph Stern

"Travel can be the best inspiration for design."
Jeffrey Bellfy

Left: Swivel glider lounge chairs and ottomans from Century Furniture fit perfectly with Swaim butterscotch leather sofas lined in silver nailhead trim upholstered in down. To mask the traditional bay window, we sheathed it in a grey-green, sheer fabric punctuated by a Century Furniture black wood circular hinged screen in the center. A six-foot-square coffee table with an inlaid raffia top anchors the room. Custom art that is also functional, like the eight-foot, lighted, bronze wall sculpture from Art Concepts Design of France, is juxtaposed against a custom-built, two-tone cherry wall unit. Panels of two-tone, iridescent fabric trimmed in braided leather are upholstered between cherry pilasters and atop a custom 25-foot, black lacquered, footed credenza with silver leaf accents.
Photograph by Joseph Stern

Above: The foyer houses an intricate wood fretwork wall hanging, stacked three-high and mounted inside a thick molded frame. Asian influences abound, from the sculpture to the fine art to the tabletop accessories.

Facing Page: The breakfast room and family room combination is indoor-outdoor living at its best. To maximize the indoor-outdoor connection, we created four distinct seating areas in the outdoor loggia and added split-bamboo header shades across the long expanse of glass that looks out over the adjacent pool and spa. The living room, breakfast room, and family room all open to the outdoors, a detail reminiscent of resort living.
Photographs by Joseph Stern

J. Edwards Interiors

Alabama

Jenny Edwards approaches design with an adroit eye for color, texture, and scale, which enables her to create rooms that appeal to a wide range of homeowners. Whether imbuing a room with bold color or choosing eclectic pieces to create a one-of-a-kind design, Jenny ensures all her spaces are both elegant and edited. She enhances a home's architectural features, which allows her rooms to appear effortless and livable. With an attention to detail that extends into every step of her process, Jenny develops designs that balance formality with comfort. The result is a relaxed environment perfect for entertaining or enjoying with family.

Left: I kept the design for a teenage girl's room sophisticated but fun. The playful lighting and thick shag carpet provide visual interest above and below the crisp, indulgent bedding. The mirrored bedside tables project a dynamic reflection, which is picked up in the silver elements throughout the room, such as the hanging pendants, vases, and throw pillows.
Photograph by Brian Francis

"Mixing traditional with modern eclectic gives the eye something to love."
Jenny Edwards

Above & Right: Wood beams add a natural element to the living room's diverse design. A modern coffee table takes center stage, while strategically placed artwork dots the layout. To give the homeowners control over the room's brightness, a panorama of neutral-toned drapes covers a large wall of windows. The reading nook provides a cheerful splash of color, and leather slipcovers provide a touch of formality without being too heavy.

Facing Page Top: Knotty white oak sets the tone in the foyer. Funky fabric patterns are an interesting contrast to the scroll-topped sofa, and a large piece of wall art provides scale between two cylindrical lighting features.

Facing Page Bottom: The white oak continues into the kitchen, this time in a ceiling application. A glass countertop and marble backsplash paired with the room's earthy tones create a fresh and inviting environment.
Photographs by Brian Francis

J. Hirsch Interior Design

Georgia

As the daughter of an architect and a watercolor artist, Janie Hirsch found interior design to be the perfect melding of her upbringing and heritage. She first worked in New York as a lighting designer, then hit the ground running in Atlanta and has since amassed more than two decades' expertise designing interiors that have garnered no small amount of national attention. Her homes are found all over the East Coast and the South, and she's been lauded with countless prestigious awards. One thing will always be consistent no matter the home's location: Janie's signature eclectic combination of classics with antiques, with furnishings situated perfectly within the architectural context. J. Hirsch Interior Design's tailored, timeless, sophisticated look charms homeowners and ages gracefully.

Left: The Neely Farm Clubhouse, originally the home of a prominent Atlanta family, now hosts events and parties for a neighborhood. Our task entailed designing a functional, classic clubhouse while restoring the farmhouse feel true to the house's roots. In the sitting area anchored by a round cocktail table, the large breakfront home to antiques from the original farmhouse era contributes to a cozy quality that invites intimate conversation.
Photograph by Chris Little Photography

"Fabric and fibers really ground a design; one swatch can inspire the whole room." *Janie Hirsch*

Above: The farmhouse–clubhouse's living and dining rooms stay true to the overall house concept while embracing a variety of potential functions. The living room, grounded by the original fireplace, contains multiple seating areas for gathering and conversation with enough open space to encourage easy guest flow and mingling. The dining room works as a place to eat or to hold meetings.

Facing Page: A space that doubles as a dining room and a music room benefits from the charcoal sheer drapery, which blends in with the wall color and makes a dramatic effect when closed for added intimacy. The silk paprika pillows add some brightness to the calm interior, a serene and comfortable spot to enjoy music.
Photographs by Chris Little Photography

"Using color, texture, or pattern as a neutral can bring a quiet sophistication to a home." *Janie Hirsch*

Right: The home's Swedish attributes extend to the grey and blue that imbue the master suite with a luxurious and calming ambience. The trim detail created panels around the room and the freestanding tub in the master bath. I chose a corner of the bedroom that looks into the bath as the perfect place for a small sitting area, and created a custom-made headboard with a heavy decorative frame moulding for the bed. The size fits perfectly between the windows and the linen upholstering complete the high dramatic backdrop.

Facing Page: The grey lacquer custom-made cabinetry with a white glaze and greywashed heart of pine floors convey cool Swedish elements and contrast nicely with the warm gold walls. The full-height cabinetry along the far wall, ready for use as both storage and pantry, packs the small space with function. In the keeping room—a gathering place for family and friends during meal preparation—we covered the brick fireplace and surround in Pastel-Cote, then painted them to achieve an older look. I carried the Swedish color palette into the kitchen-adjacent space, in contrast to the charcoal dining–music room next door.
Photographs by Chris Little Photography

"Prizing a timeless quality above all else means that these rooms have a much higher potential to be inherited and passed down to the next generation." *Janie Hirsch*

Above: I brought together warm woods, crisp linens, and eco-friendly bamboo fabrics to make a relaxed, elegant Italian-style farmhouse dining room. The setting is family-friendly, perfect for casual or formal entertaining, and shows off the owner's collection of antiques and artwork. Notable elements include the patterned flooring and custom-made plank trestle table.

Facing Page: The lady's sitting room encompasses the functions of inspiring the fashion designer owner, offering a place to lounge and read, and hosting a chat with a friend. The European palette of warm yellows and cooler greys inspired me in putting together a fashion-forward interior that is home to beautiful fabrics, furnishings, and artwork. A corner displays a wire dress sculpture crocheted from a single spool of wire, custom-made silk draperies with dressmaker details, books on famous fashion designers, and antique sewing accessories. A small niche allowed me to place a desk for a work area within it, with an exquisite silk panel as art behind.
Photographs by Chris Little Photography

Janet Bilotti Interiors

Florida

Designer Janet Bilotti, ASID, prefers to look at the big picture. Her interiors rarely simulate each other as they're each a depiction of the homeowner's aspirations and goals for the space. Rather than focusing on a particular trend or style, Janet—who maintains a Florida ID License #11—creates environments that are a sum of all the room's components, from thoughtfully appointed accents to the perfectly selected wall treatment. She meshes her homeowner's desires with the structure of the allotted space in such a way that the results are always a cohesive design without the need for any single, large, or overstated focal point.

Left: The challenge for me was to design a living room to suit both the wife, who desired an elegant and more formal space for entertaining, and husband, who wanted another television away from the family room and kitchen.
Photograph by Randall Perry

Above: A New England couple, who also has a traditional home in Boston, wanted their brand-new condo to be crisp and light. Mouldings and a coffered ceiling add finishing details while the colors, driven by the surrounding sand and sea, add appreciation to the long views of the Gulf of Mexico.

Facing Page: We planned the space for a large, open living room to include a wine tasting lounge, to accommodate the homeowner's passion while creating a space that was more open than a traditional wine cellar.
Photographs by Randall Perry

"Design inspiration comes from ever-changing influences including art, fashion, and the constant influx of new information and materials." *Janet Bilotti*

"Transitional design is like fashion. I dress classically one day and have a pair of contemporary shoes on the next day. It keeps me stimulated to think in a lot of different ways."
Janet Bilotti

Above: The project was a total renovation of a gulf-front apartment that I had previously designed 12 years earlier for the same owners, and the objective was to make it sleek and modern. The open kitchen allows the gourmet chefs to cook and enjoy their company.
Photograph by John Stillman

Facing Page Top & Middle: The homeowners desired an outdoor room that was warm and inviting for their large extended family and friends. Our use of natural textured materials, warm lighting, and comfortable "stay awhile" furnishings give both the outdoor and indoor living areas a relaxed but elegant design. Attention, as usual, was paid to lighting, scale, texture, and details.
Photographs by Dan Forer

Facing Page Bottom: The owners of this gulf-front master bedroom on a southwest Floridian island wanted their bedroom to take on the island flavor and welcome them during seasonal stays away from New England winters.
Photograph by Randall Perry

JMA Interior Decoration

Florida

Native Floridian Jacquelyn M. Armour of JMA Interior Decoration is that unique interior designer with an architect's instincts. Jackie received her interior design degree with a focus on architecture and drafting, then opened her firm in 1996 to provide South Florida with timeless, thoughtfully curated interiors. Jacquelyn grew up in a bright, art-filled home, so she brings her abundant love of color to every home while outfitting it with a clean, classic look: in her words, "Ralph Lauren meets Lilly Pulitzer." Detailed floor plans, architectural elevations, and interior perspectives for her homeowners to review during the design process are reassuring elements that complete JMA's comprehensive, meticulous style.

Left: We created a serene and sophisticated ambience for the living room by choosing classic furnishings and warm neutral textiles that relate to the beautiful antique screen. The room feels naturally derived, as if the decorative elements were collected over time through exciting world travels.
Photograph by Ron Rosenzweig

"Never underestimate the power of art. Beyond a mere focal point, it can inspire the color palette or define the whole ambience."

Jacquelyn M. Armour

Above & Facing Page: It's all about keeping a space light, bright, and airy, not overwhelmed by any one piece. One Northeastern couple's coastal retreat speaks to the Florida climate and lots of natural light. Found in New York by the homeowner, the painting functions as the focal point of the living room. We found the fun polka dot fabric for the chairs first and built from there. Neutral khaki walls play to the sophistication of the homeowners' existing mahogany pieces, while a natural sisal rug and a shell chandelier in the dining area nod to Florida in an elegant way.

Photographs by Ron Rosenzweig

"A myriad of individual elements complete a home. The artful selection and arrangement of these is the basis for all of our projects."
Jacquelyn M. Armour

Above: A Bermuda-style home characterized by soaring volume and strong architecture contrasts with the Northeastern homeowners' more formal primary residence. A refinished vintage console, tufted settee, and canvas mural depicting natural vegetation, orchids, and bamboo bring in color intensity while creating an updated Palm Beach look.

Facing Page: To temper the home's Mediterranean architecture, we installed contemporary furniture for a truly transitional feel. In the classic master bedroom, the solid, plush bed plays off the abstract movement in the painting to generate a modern upscale retreat. In the living room, a sense of restrained drama permeates the space; pale sea glass-green chairs in classic lines tie into the celadon jars on the fireplace. The entryway boasts a hand-stenciled groin vault ceiling, while a transitional-to-contemporary mirror above the console table establishes right from the start that the home goes beyond traditional Mediterranean sensibilities.
Photographs by Ron Rosenzweig

Above: Pale green walls and overflowing light lend the space a Florida spa feel. To recreate the room, we painted a gold table white, turned silver chairs brown, and changed out the entry mirrors, resulting in a very streamlined look.

Right: To our homeowner's surprise, a coat of white paint was all it took to update and enhance a pair of solid bronze console tables that flank the entryway. Custom-made mirrors above each match the paint finish, while tangerine lampshades make a fun statement.

Facing Page: To transform the library into something cleaner, fresher, and more reminiscent of Florida, we painted dark burgundy walls the color of beach sand and used embroidered pillows hand-made by artisans in Chile as the starting point for the room. The graphic statement of the rug relates to the pillow, while a modern beach scene painting and French shell watercolors on heavy parchment paper in leather frames set the tone for an updated, more modern waterfront library.
Photographs by Ron Rosenzweig

Mary Washer Designs

Florida

When Mary Washer switched majors from psychology to art during her senior year of college, she was searching for a calling that would satisfy both the artistic and the grounded aspects of her personality. A career in design was not only the practical choice, but also provided her with the opportunity to unleash her creativity on a daily basis. After several years of working on vacation homes in North Carolina, she moved to Florida, maintaining her former clientele and eventually opening her own firm. Among Florida's sultry climes and stellar views, she found a clientele rich with world travelers who not only came to the plate with a wealth of ideas but also had the energy and enthusiasm to undertake the kind of sweeping projects that make even the most grounded heart soar.

Left: In Florida, it's all about the views, so I am constantly aware of drawing the eye back toward the windows. By using silk fabric on the curtains and coastal blues in the upholstery, we are able to tell a story that connects one room to the next. From the windows to the moulding to the ceiling, we were able to maintain a consistent narrative that had one foot in traditional design and the other in soft contemporary.
Photograph by Michael Stavaridis

Above: A cozy seating area overlooks the porch to outside. Careful use of various shades of green imitates the outdoors just enough to allow the eye to travel to the window. There is a balance of modern and classic, tied together with the rustic coffee table.

Facing Page: The coastal blue upholstery adds serene color to the room. It combines traditional design with soft, contemporary design, creating an ocean ambience that flows with the painting. A shell-inspired lamp seamlessly continues with the theme.
Photographs by Michael Stavaridis

"Design is all about balance: formal and informal, color and texture, symmetry and asymmetry." *Mary Washer*

"When you travel, soak in the textures, colors, and juxtapositions and pocket them in your mind."

Mary Washer

Above: When we first saw this room, the center windows were completely obscured by an entertainment center, so removing that mammoth obstruction and opening up views to the water was job-one. In Florida, especially on the water, where you can watch the weather patterns change from the comfort of your family room, the views make the home.

Facing Page Top: Before deciding to renovate an older home, the couple had planned to build a new home in the style of the British West Indies. The bed was a perfect fit for the original plan, but it took some skill to make it—and the Italian rug—fit with the new plan. We lightened up the mood by using a faux metallic wall treatment and contemporary light fixtures that kept the room simple, not stuffy.

Facing Page Middle: Originally decked out in English country floral wallpaper and stained glass, the bathroom was screaming for a makeover. The carrara marble on the floor and cabinets allows the space to feel simultaneously traditional and contemporary, while the elegant lines of the tub add an unforgettable visual.

Facing Page Bottom: When you have a homeowner who loves cooking so much that she has travelled to Tuscany to take cooking classes, you have to make the kitchen extra special. The generous table, butcher block island, mosaic stone backsplash, and wood mantel fill the space with traditional Italian warmth.

Photographs by Michael Stavaridis

Posh Exclusive Interiors

Louisiana

Posh Exclusive Interiors' president and principal designer, Monique Breaux, believes that a successful design experience centers on creating spaces that are visually timeless and emotionally resonant. Over the past 20 years, Monique has taken her designs across the globe, lending her keen eye to homes, hotels, and more. Be it palatial estate or luscious loft, Posh commits to a project with exacting attention to detail and a true personal interest in the owners' style. When designing homes with traditional décor, Monique combines polished elegance with chic modernism. In doing so, whether the furniture is circa 1850 or the most sought after of contemporary looks; the accessories heirlooms or recent finds, the room is always comfortable for its Old World charm and new millennium sheen.

Left: For the sitting room, I chose a mix of elegant staples—the voluminous crystal chandelier, the champagne flute pedestals—and combined them with items of modern class, like the acrylic-back chairs and geographic spirals featured on the gilded mirror and stiletto club chairs. The magenta and turquoise in the room add both character and contrast.
Photograph by Chipper Hatter

Above: Stepping in from the rustic wood-paneling, the powdery kitchen exudes pure cleanliness—a brave choice for an area rife with pasta marinara and cabernets. Harmoniously repeated color swatches blend the hallway into the kitchen, as evidenced by the shared emerald and sapphire tones in the painting and fresh foliage.

Left: The gorgeous drapery sweeps the viewer away into decades past; while a foursome of colorful and cross-legged dining chairs and a glass-top table offer an artistic alternative to simpler décor.

Facing Page Top: The master bedroom suite proves that excess need not be gaudy. The king-sized tufted headboard and matching loungers nearly reach out and hug you, but the neutral colors portray subtle sophistication.

Facing Page Bottom Left: A carefully organized closet is a welcome luxury for homeowners. With sapele mahogany wood and marble countertops, even the parts of the home behind closed doors are steeped in refined taste.

Facing Page Bottom Right: The home's motif of white walls and floral arrangements extends to the bathroom. A translucent chair brings the home full circle back to the sitting room. The cleanliness of the master bath is enhanced by the reflective marble floor and clean lines that define the sink's silhouette.
Photographs by Chipper Hatter

Puschendorf Interiors

Florida

A perfectionist with an eye for timeless design, Aldo Puschendorf has been honing his creativity since his teenage years, when he realized his knack for visual merchandising at a major retail store. Transitioning to residential interior design was every bit as natural, as both pursuits require attentiveness to individuals and how they interact with their surroundings. Aldo gleans inspiration for his work in much the same way, visiting the space during the day, going back again at night, and looking to the residents' personalities and preferences. But then he completely withdraws from his studio setting for a lively cardio workout—that's when the ideas really begin to flow. It's a process unique to him that yields results as inimitable as the people who enjoy them. Whether designing from his office in Miami or his showroom floor, Aldo is forever inspired by the diversity of beautiful natural and built environments all around him.

Left: In the modern living area, the architecture's angularity guided the sparing use of furnishings and accents. One of the most effective and evocative ways to create a contemporary aesthetic infused with elements of the dramatic is through large-scale, interesting artwork, such as the environmental portrait. I love the process of guiding homeowners to select pieces of fine art that delight them—maybe the residents relate to the work on a personal level, find it amusing, or simply appreciate the composition.
Photograph by Robert Brantley

"Nothing says 'timeless' like warm neutrals, plush furnishings, and a glamorous chandelier."
Aldo Puschendorf

Above & Facing Page: My natural inclination with any design is to incorporate bold splashes of color whenever possible, but for a husband and wife who were conservative to the point of beige, I embraced a neutral palette because that is what they find pleasing and soothing. The refined quality of the interior reflects their traditional sensibilities yet the way I brought all of the elements together gives the space a very updated, slightly contemporary feel. I chose a pocketed design for the draperies because I'm a firm believer in hiding all of the hardware so that you can wander through the space without visual distraction.
Photographs by Robert Brantley

"Accent pillows are the jewelry of interior design."
Aldo Puschendorf

Above & Right: Though the Aventura, Florida, vacation property is enjoyed just a few weeks out of the year, the residents have exceptional taste and insisted on perfection with every detail. The living room is designed to have a chic downtown hotel vibe but clearly reference the beauty of its beachfront setting. Warmth and sophistication also pervade the master bathroom, which was an entirely uninteresting box until I came up with the ceiling treatments to give the room some architectural personality. My vanity design brings you back to the early days of Hollywood with its soft curves and beautiful finish; it's exactly the focal point that the space was missing.

Facing Page: With interesting design parameters that all of the angles and openings be square—rather than rounded—and that the rooms be painted a crisp white, the architect and I collaborated to design the home from the ground up, outside and in. The large dining room is made more intimate through the selection of two glass-top tables that each seat eight guests; the commissioned oil painting really defines the space. In the den, the architectural teak chairs from Artefacto are the stars of the show. They are very much in keeping with the owners' request for linear elements yet possess a certain unexpected playfulness.
Photographs by Robert Brantley

Wolfe-Rizor Interiors

Florida

Hattie Wolfe and Abigail Rizor are a mother-daughter design duo who has made collaboration an important part of the creative process. Hattie has been exploring her creativity since age 12, when she first discovered her love of and natural talent for designing. Her daughter Abby has carved out a design career of her own, putting the focus on creating spaces that reflect a homeowner's unique lifestyle. By bouncing ideas off each other, the team works in tandem to find solutions to even the most difficult design challenges. With a masterful understanding of scale, proportion, color, and texture, Hattie and Abby create livable layouts that exude their signature rustic-contemporary style.

Left: With its 1920s Spanish-French-Mediterranean milieu, the living room features modern elements but lacks the application of current trends to ensure the design stands the test of time. Designs are afforded staying power when elements remain classic and sophisticated, focusing more on the feeling of a space rather than the objects in it. The room uses industrial features to give it texture and a rustic edge, such as the antlers over the mantle and the stacked kindling near the fireplace. Proportion plays a large part in the space, with French furniture designed with a subdued scale.
Photograph by Stephen Allen

Above: People have begun eliminating the home's formal spaces and are instead leaning toward relaxed environments for eating, gathering, and entertaining. The home's bright kitchen features a neutral color palette with grey limestone floors and white walls. A baker's rack displays dishes while keeping them within easy reach, and the long harvest table is the ideal locale for enjoying a meal. The design balances classic elements with a modern twist; for instance, the white buffalo head that hangs above a black faux-alligator booth. Black Philippe Stark chairs in the nearby family room bring a sharply modern element into the open layout—and it's the incongruence between old and new, classic and contemporary that makes the overall design so successful.
Photograph by Stephen Allen

Left: While the home may be small, the cozy and sophisticated space is packed with function, and the summery ambience keeps the small area feeling spacious. The spiral staircase adds a stunning focal point in the main living area where the homeowners enjoy spending most of their time. Mohair sofas and French leather club chairs that flank an onyx-topped iron table provide plenty of seating for private meals or entertaining. A glass lamp upon the buffet is balanced by the transparent ghost chair, and the sisal rug adds hearty texture.
Photograph by Jesse Wolfe

Facing Page: In the kitchen, a large table is the gathering place for family and friends. Neutral cabinetry provided the color inspiration for the entire house, and in the kitchen, complements the industrial-looking volcanic rock countertops. Overhead, an iron Greek sponge basket—once used for collecting sea sponges in the ocean—is repurposed into a lighting fixture.
Photograph by Stephen Allen

Billy Blanco Designs

Florida

Dark and light, cool and warm, hard and soft. If juxtaposing disparate components keeps a room interesting, then spaces designed by David G. Blanco and Billy Jurberg of Miami-based Billy Blanco Designs are exceptionally interesting. Blending natural elements with pieces that reflect contemporary sensibilities, David and Billy create rooms that delight the senses. Endowed with an exceptional sense of proportion, David and Billy embrace expansive design elements that accentuate the grandness of a room, and smaller spaces are treated with the same care and attention. The team is adept at piecing elements together regardless of inherent style, thereby creating an eclectic mix that creates a home.

Left: The onyx wall is a striking focal point for the adjacent dining room. When lit at night, the veins play across the stone in gorgeous detail. The Hudson dining table, constructed of one single piece of hardwood, projects an old-fashioned maritime feel with contemporary finishing. The high gloss stretch canvas ceiling resembles boat sails, while gauzy draperies soften the edges of the windows.
Photograph by Morris Moreno

Above: Elegant living spaces need to be practical as well as beautiful. In a room used for both entertaining and family time, separation of space is often the best way to accommodate the homeowners' various needs. A back-to-back Italian leather sofa provides a much-needed separation of the formal sitting area near the gorgeous Atlantic Ocean view, while the sectional part of the sofa encompasses the more casual gathering area.

Left & Facing Page: Design elements that allude to a seafaring lifestyle prevail throughout the home. A reposed copper table in the formal sitting area stands beside two stools which are made with threaded rope. Caribbean blue marble was used for the bar countertops, reflecting the blue of the ocean. Four chairs in the sitting area surround a natural iron tree trunk table. Pendant lights cascade from the dual-textured ceiling—one part smooth and glossy which resembles sails, the other highly grooved to mimic the movement of the clouds.
Photographs by Morris Moreno

Above & Right: Reminiscent of a pier, the foyer juts into the center of the home. The ceiling conveys a sense of movement upon entering the space, opening to the bar on the left and the kitchen on the right. Immediately, the eye is drawn to the back-lit organic onyx wall, upon which large pieces of coral—chosen specifically for the space—sit.

Facing Page: The dining table, surrounded by contemporary chairs, perfectly marries the old to the new and the rustic to the modern. Giving the homeowners a durable, family-friendly piece, the solid-wood top that graces the dining table is naturally elegant.
Photographs by Morris Moreno

Above: Sweeping views of the Atlantic are uninterrupted by the low-profile furnishings both inside and out.

Left: A custom-made limestone pedestal sink with a backdrop of white, blue, and clear glass tile—made to resemble weathered seaglass—create a stunning setting for freshening up in the powder room.

Facing Page: A sleek hallway leads to the master and guest bedrooms. Each space balances glass and wood, wood and metal, metal and glass. The combination of sleek, hard surfaces against warm, organic textures creates a harmonious balance.
Photographs by Morris Moreno

Above, Right & Facing Page: For their summer house, a Toronto family wanted a seaside-inspired, natural feel to their home. The wide-plank, ultra-long wood floors keep the tone of the room casual and organic. The Billy Blanco Design Team shopped the area to find unique local items for the décor; books and small decorative items in the living room shelves are local finds. A mid-century-inspired dining area is crowned by a pendant light featuring slips of paper with quotes written upon them, and the oversized mirror and Lucite table in the hall are from a nearby vintage shop. Linen and cotton blends on the upholstered furniture, highly lacquered consoles, glass and Lucite surfaces, hardwoods, paper, coral, and steel combine to create an eclectic beach retreat.
Photographs by Morris Moreno

Above Left: The wallpaper's pattern carries mid-century touches into the guestroom and workspace area of the home. With its soft, natural tones, the paper provides an interesting canvas for the room's furnishings without stealing too much attention.

Above Right: Situated along "Millionaire's Row," the home's terrace provides a gorgeous view of the Atlantic. Crisp white draperies and white metal patio furniture complete the clean look.

Left & Facing Page: The blue crab lamp was an item found locally by the designers and homeowner. Turquoise accents on the bed pop in the otherwise monochromatic bedroom. A vintage table made from carved wood elephant heads serves as a vanity when paired with the modern chair. Natural elements—capiz shells, linen, and wood—keep the room casually elegant.

Photographs by Morris Moreno

CAD International

Florida

When it comes to design, it's important to interiors guru Charles Allem to decipher exactly what his homeowners mean when they say "contemporary." By working with them in detail and observing their stylistic tendencies, Charles is able to produce an end result that's exactly the sort of contemporary they had in mind, from futuristically modern to warmly transitional. Inspired by everyday surroundings found in art, nature, and even fashion, Charles thrives off a minimalist environment and monochromatic design. The results, which he's often editing down to the last second, are studies in chicly modern interiors punctuated by crisp, clean accents.

Left: The city view as the sun sets over Miami is truly magical. The entire apartment, and especially the room—which we equipped with a state-of-the-art sound system and 3D television—make the Minotti sofa the perfect setting for enjoying a good movie. Construction by Jarosz Development.
Photograph by Kim Sargent

Above: The open plan layout in the living room, dining room, and bar is ideal for entertaining. The wild agate bar is quite the conversation piece, as it melds technology with nature. However, because it was built abroad and crated to the site, it was a logistical challenge—especially since we made it happen in only two months. We felt the use of fashion photography throughout the apartment was perfect for its South Beach location. The piece in the image, titled *Mask*, is by a prominent fashion photographer and was featured in *Italian Vogue* in 2006. It was shot in a studio in New York City, and the golden mask was crafted specifically for the shoot.

Facing Page: Three custom Murano glass backlit wall panels carry on the tones from the wild agate bar. The modern stairs are accented with a custom Tai Ping runner to add drama and harmonize the colors throughout the apartment.
Photographs by Kim Sargent

"Fashion can have an immense influence on design." *Charles Allem*

Above & Facing Page Top: Luxurious fabrics create a sumptuous master bedroom in which to enjoy the peacefulness of the ocean outside the sliding glass doors. Waking up to inspiring views and enjoying breakfast on the lovely terrace are a great way to start the day. Our custom millwork adds storage space while framing the television and providing a sleek desk. Although the master suite boasts a generous closet, there can never be enough storage space.

Facing Bottom: With a divine view of the beach, we designed the patio to have a minimalist effect for a relaxed setting. A touch of greenery brings a garden feel and also adds color. Chaise lounge couches are ideal for reclining in the dappled sunshine.
Photographs by Kim Sargent

"I was drawn to design from a very early age. While I was in my teens, our home in South Africa was being designed by the late David Hicks. Participating in that process assured me that my future was in this field." *Charles Allem*

Carlos Polo Interior and Lighting Design

Florida

A childhood in Columbia, a lighting education in Italy, and interior design studies in the sultry climes of South Florida have kept Carlos Polo a very busy man. At his home studio in Clearwater, he designs multi-faceted contemporary masterpieces. The music plays and the wine flows while he works—a passionate work style for a passionate man who values chemistry, a true connection with the homeowners he works with, above all. The formula works; his projects in interiors and lighting design have made him a hot commodity in locales from Harbor Island to the under-the-radar vineyards of Southern California. And no matter who the client is, he always starts with the same question: Why do you think you need a designer? If the answer is simple and true, then the rest is just details.

Left: It was important to shine a spotlight on the Tampa home's architecture while retaining the simplicity of the space. I started by creating a horizontal pattern in the focal wall, leaving gaps between the sheetrock panels. The horizontal visual planes continue along exterior windows, where sheer panels maintain the pattern and stay true to the homeowner's minimalist style.
Photograph by Frank Baptie

Above: Sleek black cabinets accented with stainless steel appliances create a minimalist effect. Grey tile adds to the two-toned palette while setting the kitchen apart from the hallway.

Facing Page: I created simple lines in the living area by placing a long glass table parallel to the crisp white couch and chairs, sitting it on a runner-style carpet. The navy blue wall accents the room, creating a focal point for the futuristic-inspired artwork.
Photographs by Daniel Newcomb

"Simplicity has a powerful effect." *Carlos Polo*

"Building is one thing, but interior design is art. And for art, you have to have chemistry." *Carlos Polo*

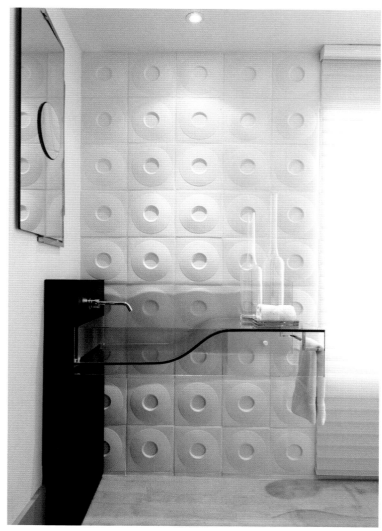

Above: The original jumble of green shag carpet, cabin timbers, and heavy stone was worlds away from the owner's contemporary vision. We both knew that if we played up the home's strengths, namely the views of lush trees and the lake, we would be able to transform it into a contemporary retreat where he could throw stylish parties or just have a cocktail in the afternoons and look out upon the lake.
Photograph by Clark Dugger

Right: I fell in love with these 1950s-style Ann Sacks tiles at first sight; pairing them with the green glass vanity made both elements even more spectacular. The large-scale French floor tile is elegance personified.
Photograph by Clark Dugger

Facing Page Top: In such a simple powder room, it's important to accent the space with touches of color. I chose a magenta chair and wall plates to add a splash against the graphite walls. By contrast, main elements that initially appear simple, like the Italian commode, are actually beautiful works of design. Its simple profile adds much needed sophistication in an unlikely place.
Photograph by Daniel Newcomb

Facing Page Bottom: The dining room wall is accented with gold cut outs that I then filled with striking white pottery. A modern, cubic chandelier acts as a sculpture, mimicked by the pieces atop the table.
Photograph by Daniel Newcomb

Collins & DuPont
Interior Design

Florida

Known for interior detailing, the team-oriented Collins & DuPont Interior Design is passionate about turning homeowners' dreams into exquisite living spaces. For over 25 years, founders Kim Collins and Sherri DuPont have devoted themselves to creating exceptional spaces that reflect the lifestyle, comfort, and interests of homeowners in current, innovative ways. In 2006, Alina Olinger began working with Kim and is now a strong and creative member of the team. With attention to line, detail, and a blended mix of texture, the Collins & DuPont designers work with architects and builders literally from the ground, up. In creating a relationship with homeowners, Kim, Sherri, and Alina delight most in that moment when the owner steps into their new living space for the first time.

Left: Amazing views beg to be accentuated. In an effort to create a gathering place with great visual impact, we kept the color palette within the natural hues of the oceanside, so that the eye is pulled out beyond the neutral laser-cut drapery panels and vast bay windows. A four-piece seating area nestled up to the Gulf view is composed of fully upholstered swivel chairs, allowing for an intimate entertainment space.
Photograph by Lori Hamilton Photography

Above: Ornamented with gorgeous original abstract paintings on wood by Miami artist Kurt Merkel, the bar takes advantage of the space by curving out into the room. Its unique undulating shape is mimicked in the freeform ceiling detail above, accented with solid sapele crown moulding to match the hand-polished, sapele wall panels of the bar. The mix of sycamore and mahogany creates a contrast between light and dark, while the shell pendant lights tie in with the other natural materials found in the home. Complete with a full-height, Sub-Zero wine cooler, television, and icemaker, the bar accommodates many guests while providing visual interest. Curved and sloped upholstered swivel barstools add a whimsical touch of softness to the overall setting.

Facing Page: In a Southwest Florida remodel, we took an existing space from bland, traditional, and cramped to an open floorplan which pays homage to its sub-tropic environment. The piano sits where the dining room was located before the renovation. The art niches—which showcase coconut wood and stone sculptures by Florida artist Adriana Hoyos—are framed by capiz shells which add texture and shimmer to the niches. Natural grasscloth material finishes the inside walls. A playful light fixture with floral disc detailing over the lacquer piano creates an eclectic focal point for the space.
Photographs by Lori Hamilton Photography

"Keeping an open mind is imperative to good design." *Sherri DuPont*

Above & Right: In the condominium remodel, we created an eclectic look, mixing contemporary elements with touches of nature throughout. The bright color palette of blues, greens, and cotton tones bring the master bedroom to life, accented with energizing pops of raspberry and tangerine. Sculptural hand-woven rattan chairs add character and tie in nicely with the clear-stained satin walnut nightstands and framed upholstered headboard. Grasscloth panels accent the applied moulding details in the ceiling, while a turquoise chest with bold organic hardware and an abstract tropical painting work together to complete the relaxing coastal retreat.

Facing Page Top: A geometric grid over scaled drywall beams adorns the ceiling, while natural stacked stones on the fireplace add warmth and texture. The custom tangerine area rug plays against the vibrant accents of raspberry and citron in the playful family room. Dark woods provide a great backdrop for displaying bright and interesting accessories and artwork. The large sectional, the oversized upholstered swivel chair for two, and a pair of open-slat-back chairs flanking the lineal flame fireplace create a welcoming gathering place for family and friends.

Facing Page Bottom: In the bedroom, the palette of orange and neutrals continues. The tangerine accent wall is playful and blends seamlessly into the adjacent tan walls. Pops of blue found in the decorative pillows and drapery hardware add another element of whimsy.
Photographs by Lori Hamilton Photography

Design Specifications

Florida

Distinctive interiors and exteriors of distinction and luxury are hallmarks of Design Specifications: a full-service design studio offering services in architectural detailing, full turn key interiors, and project management. With dedicated managers throughout the firm that specialize in specific fields, Design Specifications is a one-stop studio that makes designing a home a fun experience. Principal Wendy Kensler believes that no detail is too small and emphasizes the importance of the little things that make living in a home special. Since 1987, Design Specifications has created inventive spaces throughout the US and internationally. The firm works with several of Orlando's premier builders at Golden Oak in the Walt Disney World Resort, a one-of-a-kind luxury home community.

Left: Designed with the active homeowners in mind, the 24,000-square-foot house utilizes a linear design to complement its large size. When entering through the custom stainless steel front doors, guests pass under two sweeping arches to enter the great room. The two-story fireplace is clad in natural stone and bold wood panels. Distressed edges give the hardwood floors a rustic durability that stands up to toys and the traffic of little feet.
Photograph courtesy of Everett and Soule

Above: The kitchen is surrounded by stone and glass mosaic tile. Clusters of hanging pendants create visual interest while lighting the space. High-gloss dark wood cabinets and stainless steel accents are complemented by dramatic granite countertops.

Right: A custom glass door provides an entrance to the powder room. Made from poured and raised glass, it features swirling silver and gold accents.

Facing Page: The homeowners requested a super sexy master bedroom, and that's what they got. The pearlized leather headboard seems to float against the metal mesh curtain. Behind the curtain is a pocket in the ceiling that conceals lighting and provides even more depth for the bed's backdrop. The sitting area features sheer fabric and velvet seating. Rather than a fireplace, the spaces are divided by glass fire tubes for a visually seductive touch.

Photographs courtesy of Everett and Soule

"Precision and creativity go hand-in-hand."
Wendy Kensler

Left: The sexy wood veneer-clad staircase feels as if it floats in the air. Each step is lit, and the light fixtures resemble celestial bodies above. A glass railing with stainless steel handrail keeps the space open and provides views to the ground floor.

Facing Page: The covered patio and pool area feel like a private resort. Guests can gather around the outdoor fireplace and mounted television to watch the game while others play a game of volleyball at the adjacent court. The hot tub overlooks the pool, the fire pit, and the stone grotto beyond. A thatched roof covers the swim-up bar and teppanyaki grill, a perfect highlight for pool parties.
Photographs courtesy of Everett and Soule

Fanny Haim & Associates

Florida

Some little girls like horses and dolls, some follow celebrities and fashion. Then there are girls like Fanny Haim, who rearranged the furniture while the other girls were playing hide-and-seek behind it. As a young artist she traveled the world, sketchbook in hand, making note of architectural details and color schemes. She developed her ability to devote herself to her homeowners, leave her ego at the door, and breathe life into their dreams as if they were her own. At the end of the process, her trademark of turning over each home in photo-ready condition, with flowers in the vases and candy in the dishes, brings tears to the homeowners' eyes almost every time.

Left: Sculptural furnishings and organic textures echo the fine quality of the owners' contemporary art collection without overshadowing it. The rigidity of the tables, the ethnic-inspired pattern of the rug, the linearity of the chairs—every element adds interest and enhances the room's overarching classic modern style.
Photograph by Carlos Domenech

Above: The breakfast area's pristine aesthetic provides an ideal backdrop for the owners' vibrant art collection and the apartment's lush views.

Facing Page: Beachfront chic need not be cliché. I brought in natural elements of leather, linen, and burlap for the bed and wall treatment to create a sleek, organic look. The level of luxurious detailing throughout the guest room makes visitors feel especially welcome.
Photographs by Carlos Domenech

"I love design that's sophisticated, bright, and spicy." *Fanny Haim*

"One of my signature color schemes is 'truffle,' a rich, mixable palette of sexy grays and steely blues." *Fanny Haim*

Above: In the dining area, the deep, restrained colors play exquisite counterpoint to the raw materials used in the furniture and draperies. The long banquette mitigates the need for circulation on all sides of the table, thus conserving precious square footage in the downtown apartment. Rather than the expected head-of-the-table arrangement, neatly placed chairs opposite the plush banquette draw attention to the beautiful pedestal table and offer unobstructed sightlines to the window wall.

Facing Page Top: The master bedroom at once offers serene privacy and spectacular views of the ocean. Subtle sea foam green fabric and dark chocolate woodwork create a luxuriant aesthetic.

Facing Page Bottom: To maximize the expansive wall of windows while creating a much-desired television viewing area, a built-in traces the line between the kitchen and living room and flows around the corner for continuity. Equal parts stylish and comfortable, the classic modern furnishings are not subject to trend. Interesting ceiling details and lighting fixtures unite the multifunctional open living space.
Photographs by Carlos Domenech

Left: A brilliant melding of New York sophisticated—like the owners' primary residence—and beach house casual, the refined Hamptons retreat boasts a dramatic horizontal fireplace as the living room's key organizing element. Whispers of the home's location are present in the plush pebble rug, weathered driftwood table, organic tabletop accents, and several nature-inspired pieces acquired from Urban Art in Miami.
Photograph by Carlos Domenech

Above: A set of very specific programmatic requirements ushered in the multifunctional design solution. From the cocktail table and bar area near the window, the owner can easily swivel toward the beach or toward his television while working in "command center" style. The paneled wall is made of gray wood inlaid with ebony accents, and the right side cleverly conceals a deep storage pocket.

Left: The glamorous powder room is defined by rock quartz sconces and an exquisite mosaic that looks a bit like a rug climbing its way up the wall.

Facing Page Top: Denim-colored silk walls and crisp white furnishings foster a serene, enveloping ambience for the owners' grown daughters or other special guests.

Facing Page Bottom: The wood grain and horizontal floor patterning give the kitchen a decidedly modern flair. Stucco walls, ceiling detailing, and oversized glass tube lights add interest without detracting from the sleek aesthetic.
Photographs by Carlos Domenech

"To create a truly great home, a designer must be willing to completely immerse herself in the owner's fantasies."
Fanny Haim

Above: When the couple finally went to see their apartment, which had been under construction for more than a year, they were deeply disappointed with the bathroom that the builder had provided. We chose a black granite floor with an aqua butterfly pattern, reminiscent of kimono fabric. The sculptural floating tub backs up to a dramatic stone wall.

Facing Page: In such a long, vast space, it was important to create a cozy corner, a conversation area for two. The stand-up bar is limestone clad in leather, the wall behind is quartz, and the two small tables are Chinese antiques.
Photographs by Carlos Domenech

"Designing around a theme hampers your ability to think creatively. Instead, look for inspiration in things that are eternal, like the sea and sky." *Fanny Haim*

Above & Facing Page: A dreary space with gaudy gold leaf ceilings gave way to a well-styled, eclectically furnished living area. The new look is reminiscent of a hotel the owners fell in love with while traveling through Italy. Defined by a bold array of white-on-white, stainless steel, blue, leather, linen, and dark wood furnishings, the design embraces both nautical and modern classic styles. The calculated assemblage of pieces reads as an unlikely yet fascinating conversation between eras.

Left: Contrasting white quartz and gray wood countertops define the contemporary kitchen's cooking space and dining area.
Photographs by Carlos Domenec

Michelina Mottolese
Interiors Design

Florida

Good design is the manifestation of good taste, sophistication, and comfortable living. To Michelina Mottolese, principal designer of Michelina Mottolese Interiors Design, intuitively understanding the key elements in a room is paramount to creating distinctive living spaces. Michelina's multicultural lifestyle informs her design techniques. Her formative years living in Italy and Venezuela, followed by her education in New York at Parsons School of Design have given her a diverse foundation upon which she has built her firm. With offices located in Miami and Qatar, the multilingual and multicultural Michelina is involved in every step of the design process and ensures that homeowners receive a cohesive and refined design that will improve the way they live. Her designs reflect her mantra that beauty, simplicity, and functionality should work together in harmony.

Left: Built on the beach, the Miami condominium boasts sweeping views of the ocean that demand attention. The blue recessed light in the ceiling extends toward the windows and mirrors the natural tones of the water. Sand-colored hardwoods were laid so that the grain of the wood draws the eye to the windows, swathed in sheer draperies that allow the natural light to filter inside. Shimmery fabrics on the sofas in a monochromatic color scheme provide another source of reflected light.
Photograph by Emilio Collavino

Above Left & Left: A soothing palette for everyday life brings with it the balance and serenity needed to create meaningful experiences. The monochromatic scheme with pops of color is an environment that nourishes well-being and harmony.

Above Right: There is beauty in natural materials. Contrasting hardwoods on the closet doors and the floor create a dynamic yet cohesive space. Art applied directly to the wall gives the walkway a hint of life while keeping the area clear and uncluttered.

Facing Page Top: Lighting is more than just a way to illuminate dark spaces. It's an element of design that is quietly powerful and absolutely essential. In the kitchen, light defines the separate work spaces and sets the mood for the room. Going beyond convention, light is present in the reflection of glossy cabinets, in the matte stainless accents, and in the subtle shine of the floor's finish.

Facing Page Bottom: Space, texture, light, and color are the basic components of design. By observing the negative space in a room—the parts that are left simple and clean—you create a statement in itself. Selections like a glass dining table or artwork that is part of the wall create visual interest without detracting from the overall design.
Photographs by Emilio Collavino

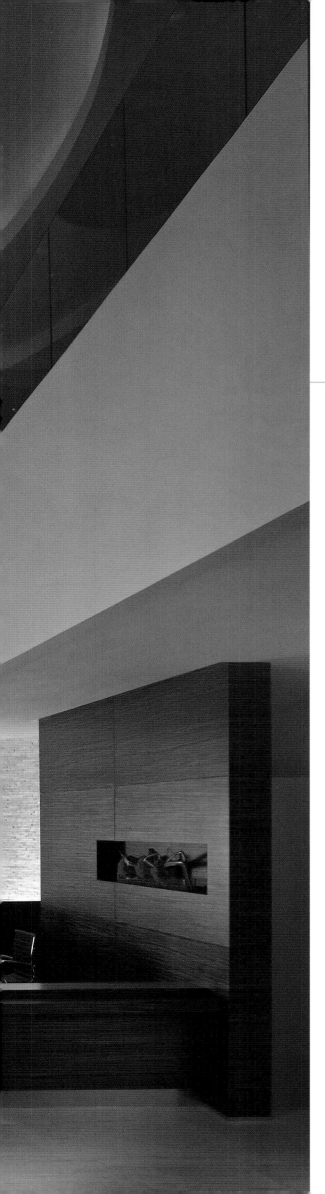

Pepe Calderin Design

Florida

Pepe Calderin fell into the design industry by fate, guided by his inherent skill for space planning and an eye for architecture. When he first started in the field, he immersed himself with the art of design, absorbing both the traditions and trends of the industry. Now his signature style is highly sought after. He combines rich elegance with warm and earthy undertones to develop highly livable spaces. Approaching each project with a keen appreciation for modernity, Pepe applies his knowledge of color, texture, and scale to originate his remarkable spaces. The result is a room that offers a lasting impression.

Left: I renovated the lobby to appear both welcoming and modern. The glass chandelier cascades from an oval-shaped ceiling, which is backed with a mirror to create the illusion of height. A pond behind the sleek oval column adds to the room's reflective elements. Onyx and wood harmonize to create the receiving desk.
Photograph by Barry Grossman

"A space has no boundaries, and has endless possibilities."
Pepe Calderin

Above & Facing Page: To create an inviting but contemporary atmosphere, I designed a wall using waved wood, which was then backlit. In the living room, lighting in the soffit above the window dramatically highlights the view of the New York City skyline without directly competing with it. Adding fiery red elements throughout the design gives it a touch of sex appeal and warmth.
Photographs by Barry Grossman

Above & Facing Page: An espresso-tone, custom-made bookcase provides niches to display vivid red and bright white elements, which add interest. The space is meant to be lounged in and enjoyed, and separate seating areas visually divide the space while maintaining the welcoming milieu. The ceiling provides a separate architectural element, displaying an asymmetrical lighting pattern to add to the design's upscale sophistication.
Photographs by Barry Grossman

"Great planning combined with a good design concept can help you create an excellent space." *Pepe Calderin*

"Lighting doesn't always need to come from above; instead, it can be woven into the design in different and creative ways." *Pepe Calderin*

Top & Bottom: A unique addition to the space, the home's red glass wall is the first of its kind. The homeowner's only request was for the color red, so I designed the wall made from both frosted matte finish and glossy glass pieces. A stunning focal point is the result, which becomes even more dynamic when backlit by strategically placed LEDs. Bottom-lit columns add to the drama and provide another source of ambient lighting.

Facing Page: With its vibrant cerulean tones, the bath is nothing short of breathtaking. Mosaic tiles line the rain shower's façade and stretch out onto the backsplash. An infinity-edge tub by Kohler takes center stage, flanked by a creamy marble surround. Dark storage spaces create contrast and hide away everyday bathroom necessities.
Photographs by Barry Grossman

Above & Previous Pages: The large living area features a gorgeous marble floor; to avoid hiding it beneath a rug, I designed a floor covering that lies in separate octagonal pieces. Each piece is held in place by Velcro, so the pattern can be easily changed when desired. A cozy seating area is positioned across from the energy efficient, ethanol-burning fireplace, which is crowned with an architectural element in frosted and mirrored glass.

Facing Page Top: The media room features a 100-inch television, which we had to bring in through the balcony by crane. Once it was mounted, I designed the wall asymmetrically—the left side of the television carries more weight than the right. I applied upholstered leather walls to counter the cold electronic elements.

Facing Page Bottom: Marble spills into the office and climbs up the walls to provide a clean elegance. Both the fireplace and hide chair warm up the space, while the contemporary lighting fixture adds a touch of unconventional beauty.
Photographs by Barry Grossman

Pfuner Design

Florida

As with most creative people, Renata Pfuner has her likes and dislikes, her favorite styles and those she'd be perfectly content to avoid. But Renata has also intentionally avoided developing a signature style, choosing instead to see each building, owner, and set of design parameters as a unique opportunity to do something fresh, amazing, and unexpected. While she is open to designing within all genres, she is most known for her glamorous modern designs infused with a distinct European flavor. Developing havens that best express their residents' aesthetics and lifestyles is no doubt an innate ability, but Renata has further enhanced the skill by regularly exposing herself to new ideas through world travels and close involvement in the design community. She views the art of interior design through a truly unique lens.

Left: Smoke and mirrors are all part of the magic in the stairway and dining area, where grey shades appear from the stainless steel on the stairway railings, to the silver leaf finish and velvet upholstery on an elegant set of dining chairs.
Photograph by Craig Denis

Above Left & Facing Page: As the heart of the home visible from virtually every room, the space needed to fascinate, amaze, and awe. Design continuity comes from repeated and reinterpreted themes; the large dining area contains high-backed chairs with a random line design we selected to keep the space active despite repetition. A palette of white, grey, and silver with some light woods, accentuated by mirrors and glass, engenders depth and drama. High ceilings and walls necessitated larger-than-life components, including the eye-catching chandelier and the mirror embedded into the stone wall.

Above Right: A white-lacquer Italian table with a mirrored inset paired with chairs that are shaped with an airy and festive cutout design suggest a bit of fun and whimsy in the breakfast area.

Right: The private elevator lobby, as the transition into the residence, functions as the first and last impression. To set the mood, I created atmosphere through white textures, ceiling designs, and varied lighting, as well as large mirrors and a grand console table. The expansive space, careful not to be too minimal, captures a certain sensation without revealing too much.
Photographs by Craig Denis

Above: The living, entertainment, and family room aims to be sophisticated and comfortable at once. Orange and yellow accent the main white tones, and the clean lines of the sectional and custom-made built-in contribute to an uncluttered but inviting space. As with other areas in the house, the ceiling received unique details and designs and a distinctive chandelier complements and adds sparkle to the room.

Left: Also a centerpiece in the home, the bar area flows with the other rooms and contains a wealth of functionality, but it also enjoys extra touches.

Facing Page: A room without texture and contrast is simply incomplete, which is why I created drama through lighting and ceiling design in the master suite. One wall of the bedroom is completely glass, overlooking the dining room, and a privacy curtain can close off the space when necessary. To maximize views and create the illusion of an endless panorama, I kept the design simple and instead found complexity in layers of details: the headboard, the lighting, the furniture, the mirrors, the vaulted ceiling, and concealed lighting. In the master bath as well, interesting textures explore new dimensions of a white-on-white palette.
Photographs by Craig Denis

William R. Eubanks
Interior Design, Inc.

Florida

History buffs, world travelers, and interior designers Bill Eubanks and Mitch Brown are passionate about creating the kinds of rooms that you never want to leave: beautiful, well-appointed, and, perhaps most importantly, comfortable. Even with their most contemporary projects, they find themselves looking to the past for inspiration, asking what worked really well then and how it can be reinterpreted for modern tastes and lifestyles. With offices in New York, Palm Beach, and Memphis and a loyal following that takes them across the country and internationally, it's no wonder that this style-savvy duo has mastered projects of all scopes and styles.

Left: The dining room uses organic textures on our personally designed, stretched and laminated goatskin-parchment table. A neutral palette and clean lines allow for the outside marsh to become a main focal point, marrying the interior with the outdoors.
Photograph by Kim Sargent

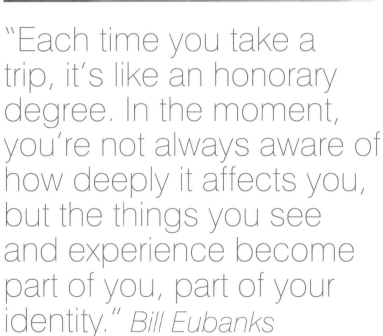

"Each time you take a trip, it's like an honorary degree. In the moment, you're not always aware of how deeply it affects you, but the things you see and experience become part of you, part of your identity." *Bill Eubanks*

Above Left: Our process of reinventing what was a very traditional condo began and ended with the beautiful marsh setting. The master bedroom is defined by our design for the Mondrian-like headboard, which our workroom team fabricated with a green raw silk and a reptile-inspired textile, a perfect complement to the natural landscape's color palette. The rock crystal lamp—one of several throughout the home—further connects the design to the earth and serves as a visual expression of the residents' spirituality.

Above Right: A nod to Southern sleeping porches of yesteryear, the loggia doubles as a casual lounge area and sleeping quarters for the residents' grandchildren. The relaxed open-air living space really embodies the desired vacation feeling.

Facing Page: The parchment walls, polished iron railing, bird's-eye maple woodwork, and infinity mirrors combine for an unexpected yet delightful effect. When you first arrive in the space, it takes you a few glances around the room to figure out why it looks and feels so good.
Photographs by Kim Sargent

"Design far from trends; aim for timeless and contemporary." *Mitch Brown*

Above, Right & Facing Page: Originally a highly traditional environment with crown mouldings and cumbersome casings galore, the space now has a glamorous vintage Hollywood look in keeping with the residents' fashion-forward sensibilities. Subtle circle and square motifs make their way throughout the home—doors, furnishings, and fixtures—for a refreshing sense of cohesiveness. Our concept is a take on the Art Deco notion of distilling beautiful shapes to their purest form.
Photographs by Kim Sargent

JJ Interiors, page 411

Plush Home, page 491

Barbatelli Signature Interiors, page 509

Exquisite Kitchen Design, page 453

west

Burbridge Design Group

California

An interior design sensation at home in Southern California and abroad in mainland China and Europe, Burbridge Design Group has gained a distinctive reputation. A lifelong lover of the fine arts and an artist, Julie Burbridge founded the Laguna Beach firm in 1981. Each project is custom-designed from the front door, including custom tile and cabinetry, furniture, pillows, bedding, and draperies. The detail-oriented approach results in nothing less than lovely, inviting, masterfully edited rooms. In 1992 Julie began designing tableware for such industry giants as Grazia of DeRuta, Italy, Sasaki, Christian Dior, and Mikasa. In 2009, she opened studio julie b. to provide the Chinese consumer market with a range of interior furnishings that matched those seen in the model homes she'd been designing in China since 2002. With interiors and custom products by Burbridge from Laguna Beach to Shanghai, San Francisco to Beijing, the firm's appeal truly transcends cultures.

Left: Casual elegance and extraordinary attention to detail characterize the beautiful coastal home; it's quite the relaxing and comfortable hideaway. A color palette of marine blue, resort white, mandarin, and wet sand celebrates the oceanfront environment.
Photograph by John Bare

"Design is a process, and throughout the development we address every part of the project; as most design professionals would agree, it's all in the details." *Julie Burbridge*

Left: In the beachfront home, the juxtaposition of elements and details, including the grouping of carefully curated collections, creates a relaxed intimacy.

Facing Page: I entered the Chinese interior design industry after a Chinese design magazine printed photos of my work in American model homes. Since then, I've designed model homes in high-end residential housing developments in numerous cities, including the Oak Bay project in Shenyang. Both the living room and the art collector's gallery represent my ability to blend Chinese cultural sensibilities with American-style interior design.
Photographs by John Bare

Above & Left: Originally built in 1928, a historic English cottage desperately needed repair and renovation. After redesigning the floor plan completely while keeping the original building envelope, a fresh and innovative version of the cottage came to life. The sophisticated interior complements the homeowner's antiques and collectibles from travels abroad. The living room demonstrates the sense of casual elegance found throughout the home. Layering a contemporary animal skin fabric, a rustic woven ikat, and sensuous velvet results in an eclectic and unexpected interior imbued with richness and texture. The small powder room became a treasure after I sought out an antique from the same time period and converted it into a vanity. I brought new life to the environment while respecting architectural integrity by blending authentic antiques with unexpected pieces.
Photographs by John Bare

Facing Page: The beach cottage, first built in 1907, required a complete reconstruction while following the local historical society's strict guidelines. To preserve that integrity, I sourced reclaimed wood flooring dating to the same era as the cottage from a North Carolina manufacturing facility to set the proper rustic, antique tone. In the living room, an invisible recessed channel was added to the top of each original beam to provide uplighting to highlight the ceiling and beams at night. I added antique light fixtures for proper illumination. The kitchen blends state-of-the-art fixtures with classic cabinetry and timeless stone materials.
Photographs by Jeri Koegel

Above & Facing Page: In one model home in the Vancouver Forest project in Beijing, the living room, private meeting room, and entertainment bar function as elegant examples of how to blend traditional American design elements with Chinese culture.
Photographs courtesy of Burbridge Design Group

"I love beginning with a blank slate and developing a design that is a reflection of the homeowner."
Julie Burbridge

"I initiate the design process by taking measure of the existing architecture and the homeowners' personalities and desires, then I begin the design development."
Julie Burbridge

Above: In a hillside Laguna Beach home, we converted the storage area under the staircase into an intimate wine cellar to house the owner's wine collection despite limited space; the antique Chinese carved doors provide the perfect finishing touch.

Facing Page: A palette of earth tones warms the space while natural linens and textured solids contribute a sense of depth.
Photographs by John Bare

Djuna & Djuna
Design Studio

Colorado

Like many couples who share a passion, Karen and Jeffrey Moore longed for a way to work together while staying true to their professional passions. Jeffrey held a fine art degree from Cooper Union and was the founder and director of The Blue Star Art Space, one of San Antonio's most revered nonprofit arts institutions. Karen owned and directed two galleries—one specializing in contemporary art and the other in international folk art. As they planned a life together, they knew that they wanted to stay in the design world but expand out of the gallery scene. Modeling their design business on one run by a couple they knew from their years in Texas, they incorporated art, art appreciation, world travel, and togetherness, and named the company after Djuna Barnes, the 1920s Parisian writer known for being a well-read, globetrotting oddball. Together Karen and Jeffrey create interiors that result in layered, eclectic, enviable spaces in Colorado and beyond.

Left: Adding coffered ceilings to a home in the Hummingbird Lodge in Bachelor Gulch transformed a standard room into an Old World hideaway. Built-ins by the fireplace, nailhead trim, and a few kitschy mountain elements combine to make guests feel fully immersed in the West.
Photograph by Kent Pettit

"Think of your space as
a gallery for your own
one-of-a-kind objects,
each with its own story."
Karen Moore

Above: When an Icelandic couple purchased a penthouse at The Ritz-Carlton, Bachelor Gulch, they requested a sophisticated, European-inspired mountain look. We went for warm and worn leathers and fabrics, down cushions, and a vintage palette of soft greens and umbers. We added a grand piano to encourage the wife's budding talent and hung snowshoes and a kayak on the walls for fun. The nine-foot, custom-forged iron chandelier took a full crew and a hydraulic lift to install, but was worth every ounce of manpower.

Facing Page: A five-foot-tall chandelier, made by a local artisan who scours the wilderness in search of naturally shed antlers, brings mountain perfection to The Ritz-Carlton, Bachelor Gulch penthouse.
Photographs by Kent Pettit

Above & Facing Page Top Right: The main level in The Terraza at Villas Del Mar at Palmilla is raised so that the views reveal nothing but ocean. Such a dramatic panorama called for a sophisticated palette of creams and dark wood. The painting at the base of stairs, which helped dictate the color palette, is authentic Spanish Colonial dating from the late 1700s.

Facing Page Top Left: At The Casita in Villas Del Mar at Palmilla, indoor-outdoor living is a breeze thanks to custom doors that fully retract into the exterior walls. Bright aquas and reds, alongside Spanish Colonial columns and rock walls, blend perfectly with antiques that I collect during my travels through Mexico.

Facing Page Bottom: The owners of The Casita maximized their second-story guest space with queen beds decked out in bedding and linens that we designed. We also designed the El Corazon iron bed frames, named for the repeating heart pattern on the rails, and grounded the room with octagonal Saltillo tiles.
Photographs by Kent Pettit

"The best homes are full to the brim with out-of-the-ordinary bits and pieces that you've accumulated throughout your life." *Karen Moore*

Ginger Atherton & Associates

Washington

Many designers tell a home how it's supposed to look, but not Ginger Atherton. Dubbed "Queen of All Things Italian," Ginger has a far more romantic approach to interior design: When she walks through the door, the home speaks to her, she listens, and every design decision she makes is to enhance the relationships between interior, architecture, and locale. Wherever the home, whatever the style, however unique the homeowners' requests, Ginger always finds a way to incorporate elements that evoke the love of life and reverence for food and family that are so ubiquitous in Italian culture. While most known for her signature approach to staging multimillion-dollar homes in Southern California, Ginger began her prolific career in the traditional field of interior design and is actively engaged in setting the stage for people's luxe lives to unfold.

Left: A grand estate in true Italian style, Casa Montecito opens up to seven acres of pristinely manicured formal gardens. Between the iron gates and the front door is a gracious rotunda capped by a 30-foot bell tower. Large-scale furnishings hold their own with the grand architecture, and paired with ambience-setting details like the scent of lemon trees wafting in from the garden, Italian candies in crystal dishes, and flickering candles throughout the home, you feel like you're in another world here.
Photograph by John G Wilbanks Photography

Above: Located between a wine cellar and a formal wine garden, accessed via either side of the grand stairway, the dining area has wonderful flow for entertaining. Texture and tonality, from the Venetian plaster walls to all the furnishings, give the space a sensual feeling. The table strategically seats six, because that's the magical number for enjoying intimate conversation at a dinner party. Any fewer and it's just dinner, any more and the group inevitably splits into two conversations.

Left: Casa Montecito's strong architectural elements carry throughout the home and are especially evident in the kitchen's massive island, stone range hood, and monolithic slabs of marble—yes, marble, it's a wonderful choice when you simply know how to care for it.

Facing Page: The master bedroom is a true sanctuary where worldly cares are left at the door. The Feng-Shui-inspired Kwan Yin statue is a lighthearted nod to one of my life philosophies. Tasteful furnishings and décor, plush carpeting, Egyptian cotton bedding, subtle scents, soft lighting from several sources—everything comes together to reinforce the notion of a personal retreat. The canopy bed is made all the more enveloping with velvet-on-lace antique draperies, rich and gorgeous, not too heavy.
Photographs by John G Wilbanks Photography

Don't do
Doormat

Above, Left & Facing Page: The Cape Cod-style home overlooks Lake Washington, so connecting the interior with the outdoors was an important design consideration. Despite the challengingly small rooms, each space feels grand with properly scaled furnishings, interesting antiques, and a few dramatic pieces like the 12-foot Coromandel screen to really set the tone. The design reflects a lifestyle of well-traveled residents who appreciate Asian culture and décor.
Photographs by John G Wilbanks Photography

"The most gracious thing a hostess can do is have good lighting." *Ginger Atherton*

Left: Designing around architectural built-ins can be rather restricting—I personally feel that they belong exclusively in kitchens and libraries—but when they are central to the home's style and detailing, you simply respect the architecture and design complementarily. The Clyde Hill, Washington, home's freestanding furnishings may be minimal in number, but they are important in style. Taking cues from the breathtaking *Madonna and Child*, I chose a crimson red to bring the living room to life. The right pops of color can do wonders for even the most ordinary spaces.
Photograph by John G Wilbanks Photography

"I want my fabrics to scream 'touch me!'"
Ginger Atherton

Above: I believe that a room is well-designed when the aesthetic is spot-on and when you know exactly how to behave in it. Clad in French walnut and designed to emphasize a portrait of the family matriarch, the formal library dictates intellectual conversation, meaningful exchanges with friends and loved ones.

Facing Page: The home's open layout is wonderful for entertaining, especially because each of the spaces has a defined purpose yet all of the spaces relate to one another. Coffered ceilings, florals mixed with deep reds and browns, and a pervasive warmth define the living areas.
Photographs by John G Wilbanks Photography

"Italians aren't interested in practical. They believe in romance and beauty."
Ginger Atherton

Top Right: The bedroom's cool, clean, refreshing design is a response to the home's breathtaking views of Lake Washington.

Bottom Right: The powder room's hand-blown glass washbowl furthers the interior's Italian flair while nodding to the artisanal traditions of the home's Pacific Northwest location. I love how the natural-edge stone vanity top marries the best of old world and new world design.

Facing Page: As the new Mediterranean-style home shows, it is entirely possible to have both high-end style and comfort that beckons guests to stay awhile.
Photographs by John G Wilbanks Photography

JF Design

Colorado

Growing up, Jane Freking found herself drawn to what looked good in a room, what colors would work best, and quality design in general. As the principal of JF Design, Jane imparts her trademark elegance and energy to high-end residential, commercial, and hospitality interior design. Her talent extends to all vernaculars, including the most traditional and Old World styles. Jane puts a great deal of effort into getting to know her homeowners intimately, and once that rapport is established, she's able to read their needs and source furnishings and accessories on instinct that are sure to be in line with their tastes. Sophisticated, unique, tailored environments characterize JF Design interiors.

Left: Hardwood floors, elaborately painted soaring ceilings, wood beams, and a stone fireplace surround define the great room. I hung a 17th-century historic tapestry to function as a focal point next to custom-made sofas upholstered in Coraggio Textiles' fig stria with silk bullion fringe.
Photographs by Ron Ruscio Photography

Above: The golden pyrolave counter, made in France and resembling ancient crackled glazed pottery, grounds the kitchen. Anchored on top of a soft paprika-painted island, it acts as the centerpiece of the space.

Right: I believe every well decorated home needs a staircase chandelier as a focal point. The custom-made sconces and chandelier of iron, stone, and crystal beads illuminate a curved entry stair and needlepoint runner while adding to the eclectic Old World mix.

Facing Page Top: An Emanuel Morez custom-made Palladio table fills the elegantly appointed dining room. Silk drapes, artistic chairs, wood beams, and painted ceilings frame the space.

Facing Page Bottom: A stunning upholstered headboard and bench, Rodolph velvet window treatments, and silk fabrics lend the master retreat warmth and opulence.
Photographs by Ron Ruscio Photography

Above: Reminiscent of a French countryside château, the gracious residence combines luxury and design with Old World craftsmanship. The home exudes elegance and comfort with carefully chosen and commissioned fabrics, rugs, and Ebanista furniture.

Left: I used Lee Jofa fabric for window treatments to give the two-story study a backdrop. The Ralph Lauren chairs, leather sofa, and sisal rug infuse the space with warmth and masculinity.

Facing Page Top: In the master bath, I chose contrasting finishes—mixing timeworn dore royal limestone with calacatta gold-honed marble and handmade Brittany and Coggs ceramic tiles—to complete the space. The Schonbek chandelier and Edgar Berebi cabinet hardware adorn the room like jewelry.

Facing Page Bottom: The kitchen's reclaimed French pavers and hand-made Tabarka tile bring together its French aesthetic; the space radiates elegance and comfort and sets the tone for the whole home's design concept.

Photographs by Ron Ruscio Photography

"I want every space to exude luxury." *Jane Freking*

JJ Interiors

Colorado

Though she started off as a chemistry major, Jennifer Jelinek, ASID, of JJ Interiors soon realized her passion was better fulfilled through the science and problem-solving aspect of interior design. With a well-honed ability to apply creative solutions to homeowners' decorative desires, she's able to develop detailed atmospheres and environments refined by comfortable surroundings. Jennifer, who also received her certificate from the National Council for Interior Design Qualification, conducts a careful dialogue with each homeowner, remaining extremely cognizant of their individuality. Her designs are completely motivated by their personality, styles, and desires, therefore each project differs from the last. However, Jennifer is often inspired by elements of nature, art, fabrics, textures, or colors to capture a versatile roster of interiors in stylishly traditional settings.

Left: By using a large three-tiered chandelier to fill up volume and placing furniture in smaller arrangements, we were able to create an inviting space. We pulled in colors that would traditionally be found in an older farmhouse; a red barn outside provided inspiration for some of the color palette.
Photograph by Ron Ruscio

"It's important to have the ability to be versatile, to specifically design for individual homeowners who have tremendously varying needs and design styles; being a kind of chameleon is essential to good design."
Jennifer A. Jelinek

Above: One of the challenges for this bathroom was to make each vanity area individually unique while balancing both masculine and feminine qualities. We had the mirrors, the center cabinets, and the vanities custom-designed and built out of renewable wood. His was more masculine and hers was curvier and feminine, but they still balance out in the room.

Facing Page: We wanted to integrate texture and natural materials, like the wood beams, the over-grouting on the stone fireplace, and the reclaimed barn wood paneling. Because it's a two-story space and is viewed from two different angles, we needed to make sure that all the details were designed so that they were interesting from every vantage point. Creating a sense of intimacy with a cozy seating group and a formal dining room also helped accommodate for the spaciousness.
Photographs by Ron Ruscio

Above & Right: Because the kitchen and bar open up to the large great room, creating a cozy, comfortable farmhouse ambience and worn-in look was important. We used distressed green antique painted cabinets on the island and custom-designed handpainted, weathered-looking tiles. The bar—complete with chicken wire inserts in the cabinets—became a great entertainment area. The wine barrel was used not only as a decorative element but also to extend the bar for additional seating.

Facing Page: Because so many windows punctuated the room, we wanted to take advantage of the views. Eliminating bulky window treatments and carefully selecting airy light fixtures allowed us to create an intimate, yet formal dining room where nature was integrated into the interior.
Photographs by Ron Ruscio

Wesley-Wayne Interiors

Texas

Using their expertise to hand-select timeless fabrics, tasteful furnishings, and unique accessories, designers Carl Wesley Lowery and Cody Wayne Glover create rooms that parallel the personalities of each homeowner. The duo often fuses traditional styling with more modern features to achieve a dynamic design. Their use of upscale elements never sacrifices quality, which allows them to transform empty square footage into inspired designs that stand the test of time. Balancing the layout by developing designs in layers, while combining a refined assortment of furniture and fabrics, they create environments that are both elegant and functional. Together, Carl and Cody are known for practical layouts that offer superior comfort, style, and beauty.

Left: In a 10,000-square-foot home, it was of the upmost importance to implement the proper use of scale throughout the design. An original 8-foot-by-10-foot painting of the Italian coast gives depth and prominence to the foyer while emphasizing the home's elegant Mediterranean influences.
Photograph by Dan Piassick

Above: Soft earth tones and comfortable materials transform a master bedroom into an inviting retreat. Blending classic styling with modern technology, the space features motorized window treatments with both sheers and blackouts for multiple levels of privacy. Expertly appointing furniture throughout the layout ensures the large space doesn't appear too overcrowded or too spare.

Left: A large-scale pattern on the powder bath's wallpaper gives the room importance. The result is a dynamic and inspiring space for guests to refresh.

Facing Page Top: From ceiling to wall to rug, each area of the formal dining room received careful planning and preparation during the design process. Dramatic silk window treatments complement the scale of the tall ceiling. The dining space exudes an opulent ambience without appearing too overbearing.

Facing Page Bottom: Oversized custom furnishings are used to complement both the interior space and the sprawling view of a private lake. The custom 10-foot sofas are gorgeous, but also provide the comfort needed to accommodate the most discerning guests.
Photographs by Dan Piassick

"The proper use of
scale and furnishings
can give any space a
strong presence."
Cody Wayne Glover

Above: Outdoor draperies provide a resort feeling in the exterior living space. They also lend a softness that helps subdue the hard surfaces of the architecture. The space is just as functional and cozy as an indoor room, using weather-resistant fabrics in lovely colors and patterns to create an environment for entertaining near the swimming pool.

Facing Page Top: The parlor's original architectural features, such as an angled fireplace, a bookcase, and plenty of glass facades, provided an interesting design challenge. In order to accommodate an unconventional arrangement, a 12-foot-round rug provides the ideal stage for the furnishings. The curved sofa also softens any hard edges and fits perfectly into the centered seating area.

Facing Page Bottom: The great room provides a multifunctional space for casual dining, lounging, and enjoying the television. A careful selection of drapery design frames the windows perfectly without detracting from the view of the private lake beyond.

Photographs by Dan Piassick

The Wiseman Group
Interior Design

California

Paul Vincent Wiseman has been a legend in San Francisco design circles since he founded The Wiseman Group in 1980. It's his knack for seamlessly combining a keen business sense with free-flowing creativity and a deep understanding of how spaces work that makes him such a luminary among his clientele. Naturally drawn to art history and architecture, Paul loves to utilize his talents and unite with homeowners to put together interiors that are appropriate to both architecture and lifestyle. Thoughtfully custom-designed pieces are another hallmark; each custom-made item is unique, not reproduced for another home. The judicious use of one-of-a-kind antiques is another way every home achieves distinction. Paul and his talented team are fluent in all vernaculars, so each home is the result of a true collaboration, which involves careful listening, as well as some intuition about what the space needs.

Left: In a 1912 summer house meant for relaxing and reading, the octagon table functions as a central sculptural piece in the small dining room, and a true dining room table when the chairs pull out. Specially reproduced by the granddaughter of renowned British architect Sir Edwin Lutyens, who designed it to reside in the Viceroy's House in Delhi, the walnut table with Brunschwig & Fils seat fabric makes an impressive statement. Other details include fumed oak floors, bronze doors with hardware we designed, two 18th-century Japanese incense burners in the shape of spotted deer, and a pair of Han dynasty pots, one bronze and one clay.
Photograph by Matthew Millman Photography

"I like to use antiques from any time period. Whether old or new, unique objects set us apart."
Paul Vincent Wiseman

Above & Facing Page: I gained deep inspiration from the summer houses on the Bosporus at Istanbul for my own summer home, because the goal of relaxation and the waterfront setting are so similar to the Bay Area location. In homage to Turkish sofas—the first invented—the rooms have a series of daybed-style sofas. The Munder Skiles furniture and French limestone floor tiles emphasize the loggia's grey-and-white palette, accented by the yellow Holly Hunt fabrics. Indian marble trays, an antique vessel from Indonesia, and a succulent to suit the Mediterranean climate finish off the serene outdoor living area, crowned by a cedar trellis.
Photographs by Matthew Millman Photography

Above & Right: A two-room San Francisco pied-à-terre acts as a city hideaway for one couple with a Northern California estate as their primary residence. The living room looks out to the Pacific Stock Exchange, so we placed only one long window seat and a bookcase along that wall to facilitate the architectural view, while simplifying and maximizing seating in the small space. To play on a slightly Moorish theme, we designed the banquette sofa, complete with fretwork panel, and the hanging lantern; the tables from Therien reflect the theme as well. An antique Khotan carpet inspired the color palette, while an antique Roman bust and a Greek oil vessel complete the look.

Facing Page: My summer house living room showcases a range of custom-made pieces and antique treasures from a mix of cultures, which all blend to create a comfortable elegance. We designed the sofas to be all-green, with unprocessed wool instead of foam filling, and undyed linen fabric, and we also crafted the light fixtures, part of our Reed Lighting line by The Wiseman Group through Phoenix Day. The 300-year-old English Jacobean chairs covered in boarskin leather, an antique rosewood tray from Indonesia, a 500-year-old Ming dynasty lacquer coffee table, a Chinese three-point vessel from the Warring States era, and the 19th-century Japanese Meiji-era reticulated lobster, made by armor craftsmen, harmonize and balance one another in the space.
Photographs by Matthew Millman Photography

A Greathouse Interior Design

Colorado

Love your home. That's the overarching goal Cynthia Greathouse has for every person who seeks out her design expertise. She knows that interior design is an intensely personal endeavor, so when she creates the environments in which memories will be made, she focuses diligently on the lifestyles, needs, and desires of the people who will live there. The effect of chiaroscuro—the interplay of light and shadow at varying times of the day—has also always fascinated Cynthia. Different levels of light create luminous interiors that sparkle and visually expand the space, a technique that Cynthia employs to ensure her clients and their homes always look their best. The spectacular Colorado landscape, including its abundance of natural light and color, is a major source of inspiration for her. Choosing a blend of colors rather than precisely matched hues, Cynthia produces rooms that evoke luxury while functioning beautifully in day-to-day life. The result is homes that are gracious and timeless, welcoming and comfortable. Cynthia's philosophy is that home should be the place you anchor your soul.

Left: One of my rules is to choose and grade colors the way they are found in nature. For example, a tree isn't made up of just one color of green; there are myriad tones and shades that all work together to create a lush and varied presentation. In a dining room grounded in a warm umber base, the soft plaid chairs and rich wood tone of the marble-topped buffet build upon the palette without disappearing into the wall color. Color, texture, and light all work together, rounded out by the gold-leafed mirror, crystal chandelier, and glass tabletop. They reflect light from the expansive window throughout the day and add sparkle into the night. *Photograph by Arthur Silk, Arthur Silk Photographyy*

Above: Leather sofas and a pair of oversized club chairs in a menswear suiting fabric are grounded by the large, French grey-blue green rug. The coffee table, made from a variety of rich woods, unifies the tones in the room. A fire crackles in the limestone fireplace, which contrasts beautifully against the warm wood. This creates a visual and textural balance when paired with the creamware displayed in the stately built-ins.

Facing Page Top: Light should not only be flattering to those in the room and establish a luminous ambience, it should also be functional. The kitchen provides ample task lighting that's balanced by the romantic swirls of wrought-iron chandeliers. The contrast of tropical green granite countertops and fresh cream cabinets creates a warm and inviting space where family and friends love to gather among the delicious aromas of holiday feasts.

Facing Page Bottom: I love to use tailored furnishings along with casual elements that knock down the formality, making a home feel luxurious but fresh. Cherished antiques add a timeless patina. Classic architectural elements and carefully chosen art pieces work together to create an intriguing presentation. Texture is a primary ingredient. I look at spaces creatively, drawing on many years of design experience and paying close attention to detail in order to infuse each space with the very essence of those who live there.

Photographs by Arthur Silk, Arthur Silk Photography

Amirob Interiors

Colorado—Arizona

Amirob Interiors has no house style, no signature look. At the Denver-based firm, everything revolves around the homeowner's personality and style. Amirob prizes synthesis—between homeowner and design team, between the design team itself. All work closely together, side-by-side, consulting on every detail no matter how minute. The only design element owner Mickey Ackerman and his tight-knit team personally see to is relevancy. Every light fixture and furniture choice must take scale and purpose into account. As long as the design has relevance, whether it's fashioned in a contemporary, transitional, or timeless aesthetic has no bearing.

Left: In the private residence located in the 2006-added Frederic C. Hamilton Building of the Denver Art Museum, the extremely open architectural space posed a real challenge that became a fantastic opportunity to create a functional, attractive kitchen. To accomplish that feat, we chose a rough-saw wingad wood that would appear like fine furniture and become a part of the architecture. Overlays in the opposite grain direction add tremendous interest. The countertop, from Germany, is the result of pressing cardboard to make a surface as hard as granite yet incredibly green. The top floats on a stainless steel formation in the same triangular shape as the museum itself.
Photograph by Eloy Minjarez

Above: Throughout the entire museum residence, no wall is straight, posing a particular challenge in the home styled with the concept of serenity in mind. The Chihuly-like 106-piece hand-blown chandelier functions as the key element in the dining space. We chose it to cast a lot of light and act as a point of interest, while making sure it didn't compete with the surrounding art collections.

Facing Page: Upon entering, an 800-year-old Buddha grounds the comparatively newer construction. The walls of the entire residence, painted with eight layers of serene tones, act as an unobtrusive backdrop for the art.
Photographs by Eloy Minjarez

"The most crucial step in the design process is listening." *Mickey Ackerman*

"Interior designers should be guides, navigating the homeowner's relationship with architect and builder as well."
Mickey Ackerman

Above: The guest bedroom continues the calm vibes, thanks to the tranquil walls and properly showcased art.

Facing Page Top: The home's great room encompasses 2,300 square feet: living, dining, kitchen, and entry. From the sofas, guests and residents can view the truly amazing Denver Art Museum architecture from 11-foot glass panels. The large open space contains many eclectic art pieces, which we positioned so that they would look as solid as the furniture.

Facing Page Bottom: When not traveling, the homeowners enjoy watching television in the secondary sitting area. We were tasked with merging collections of Greek, Italian, Egyptian, and Spanish heritages.
Photographs by Eloy Minjarez

Armijo Design Group

Colorado

For Beth Armijo, a freshly designed space is a thoughtful conglomeration of both old and new. The spirited interior designer believes that a truly comfortable environment embodies the perfect concoction of classic elements that can withstand the test of time along with items that infuse a touch of modern sensibility. Armijo is able to source inspirational ideas for texture, fabrics, color palettes, and more from activities like art and traveling. She often combines a mixture of finishes such as lacquered surfaces peppered with more natural-looking pieces, as well as light color schemes punctuated by darker well-placed accent hues. This practice provides her homeowners with truly transitional spaces that strike a balance between the traditional and contemporary.

Left: Color and texture were our main focus in the bold dining room, and the inspiration stemmed from the homeowner's love for texture and bold patterned fabric. In order to impart balance, the room needed a soft but more saturated paint color; adding the fun graphic floral art maintains the scale and keeps the eye moving. The traditional furniture pieces are redefined with the bold fabrics, keeping the room visually interesting.
Photograph by Kimberly Gavin Photography

Above: The formal living room needed a floorplan that would easily allow traffic into the study. We added a circular rolling ottoman as a comfortable footrest, but it is also easy to maneuver around. The colors also reflect transition as they draw guests through the space. Wonderful art makes both rooms a destination.

Left: Nurseries need to be functional, interactive, and flexible. I painted the custom art and made wall frames out of recycled millwork, allowing the art to be interchangeable and able to grow with the child. The color is stimulating without being overbearing, but it's still flexible for whoever uses the space.

Facing Page: Saturated with strong outdoor light, the breakfast nook is part of the kitchen but still needs to have its own identity. The traditional furniture pieces mixed with a modern chandelier, turquoise leather seats, and sheer window treatments trimmed in silk soften the strong light and create a unified but distinct space.
Photographs by Kimberly Gavin Photography

Above: Providing a thoroughfare to the kitchen, family room, nook, and basement, the space anchors the house but was large and undefined. Through the traditional architectural elements that we added, like the brick wall, fire box, ceiling beams, and classic mantel, the furniture layout and design fall into place. The fun of his-and-her Donghia wing chairs upholstered in bold fabrics reinvent in a more modern way.

Facing Page Top: In a large space with intersecting beams, the homeowner needed a place for all of the standard bedroom requirements. By using a soft grasscloth as the headboard backdrop, we added a natural, warm element. The large overscale mirror reflects light into the room and defines the dressing area. The textures and scale help transition the room into a cohesive respite.

Facing Page Middle: The kitchen was originally dark, boring, and uninviting, so we knew we needed to lighten it up a bit. By lacquering the cabinets blue and adding pendant lighting, new white quartz stone counter tops, and decorative knobs and handles, the space is transformed with a classic, fresh look.

Facing Page Bottom: The room was large, open, and not well-defined, so to compensate we added balance and definition. The warm, grey-blue color selection provided a calming element, and the lights filled the tall space with scale and a focal glow. To bring in texture, we interspersed glass vases, while the natural material of the table complemented the beams.

Photographs by Kimberly Gavin Photography

"Overall, mixing old and new is what makes more of a transitional look, such as using very contemporary furniture in a traditional home to make it a little less period and a little more timeless." *Beth Armijo*

Above: Transforming a Cordillera, Colorado, vacation home into a family getaway with ample space for overnight guests required a soft touch. The homeowner wasn't interested in the state's once-typical iron-and-antler decor, so we went with a fresh take on the mountain chalet idea with upholstered headboards, clean lines, and muted tones.

Left: Artisan glass leaves spiral out from a one-of-a-kind chandelier created by Northern California custom lighting designer Emmanuel Morris. The look is cheery and bright, very mountainesque without resorting to heavy ironcast.

Facing Page Top: A two-story stone mantle in the living room is the first thing that guests see when they cross the threshold. The hearth and custom ottomans provide ample overflow seating for when the house is packed with family and friends.

Facing Page Bottom: The family does most of their casual entertaining in the lofty, walkout basement. A high-backed, striped, upholstered loveseat, commissioned from a local furniture designer, functions as both a graphic point of interest and overflow seating. Surrounding the piece with large graphic prints helps balance the scale of the room, and the rustic side table by Oly Studio provides the one ode to rusticity in the chic space.
Photographs by Kimberly Gavin

"Art, life, and travel are great things for inspiration. For example, when I see kids in crazy outfits walking down the street, it stimulates ideas for texture and fabrics. It's my job to reinvent in a fun way." *Beth Armijo*

C + A Interior

Colorado

In 2010, Conni Newsome and Ashley Larson pooled their 20 combined years of design experience and joined forces as C + A Interior through Douglas Associates Interior Design. Conni gained expert training under Melinda Douglas of Douglas Associates, while Ashley, who has an interior design degree, learned the ins and outs of the business during her eight years at John Brooks, the diamond of Denver showrooms. Together they have the design sensibilities and the industry knowledge to find the perfect solution for any space. The C + A hallmarks are timeless quality, good taste, comfortable glamour, durability, and attention to detail. Homeowners are drawn to Conni and Ashley's knack for expressing personality through furnishing choices and arrangements, resulting in a fresh, sophisticated, and classic feel no matter the style. Both ladies are very aware of layers: layering inherited treasures with newer purchases, investment pieces with vintage store finds. These clever textures bring interest and harmony to every corner and niche of a home.

Left: We brought Leontine monogrammed linens and carefully layered rugs into an expansive master bedroom; meticulous space planning was essential for such a large area.
Photograph by Emily Minton Redfield

"Transitional spaces
bridge the two worlds
of traditional pieces and
modern elements."
Conni Newsome

Above: An arched opening connects a dining area with a living and family room. We embellished the architectural finishes of both spaces and arranged the furniture to encourage traffic flow through the dining room, which also boasts mirroring lanterns and artwork vignettes.

Facing Page: Layering patterns and color transforms the small master bedroom into a soothing retreat. Fortuny pillows, a Porta Romana lamp, and cleverly curated artwork bring everything together.
Photographs by Jason Jung and Ron Ruscio

Above: A spot in the center of the dining room gave us the chance to assemble and display artifacts that express our homeowners' personalities and life. A vintage Burlwood console, large-scale lamps, and a plush stool frame a collection of books and photos.

Facing Page: A Rose Tarlow chair sits at one end of the dining room to make a small reading nook that optimizes the open corner space. Hiro Yokose encaustic paintings and a Jean de Merry nesting table complete the cozy vignette. In the adjacent living and family room, our goal was to maximize seating and unite the two rooms. A custom-made sofa, Wendell Castle chairs, a Jeup coffee table, Bergamo pillows, vintage mercury lamps, and an antique Oushak rug help achieve both objectives.
Photographs by Jason Jung and Ron Ruscio

Exquisite Kitchen Design

Colorado

The heart of the home is the kitchen, and it's Mikal Otten's philosophy that it should be both beautiful and functional. Denver-based Exquisite Kitchen Design is Mikal's way of continuing the family business—his father, a kitchen carpenter and engineer, prized precision so much that he advised Mikal to measure to an exacting 1/32 of an inch. That love of design and dedication to perfection instilled in Mikal the desire to do something creative mixed with detail and technicality. His specialty: juxtaposing styles and materials while adding a healthy dose of global architectural influence. Mikal and his team offer Colorado residents carefully measured, exquisitely detailed kitchens filled with clever solutions.

Left: Viewing the space as tabula rasa, we completely renovated a nonfunctional kitchen and small walk-in pantry belonging to a house built around 1990 purchased by a family of five. In conjunction with interior designer Beth Armijo, we created small focal points to make the space feel comfortable. The left island, designed as a clean-up area, has been positioned close to the microwave and fridge, while the right island with its walnut endgrain butcher block acts as more of a prep zone. Tidal white leathered granite countertops, white oak floors, and walnut island cabinetry and cabinet interiors all pose an excellent contrast of browns and greys, cool and warm.
Photographs by Emily Minton Redfield

Above & Right: To replace the breakfast area that had occupied the space, we designed an island with bar stools. The walnut legs of the bar are custom-turned, with nickel caps on the bottom to contemporize them. On the other side of the island, a washing-up area hides slightly out of sight. Behind the island, one fridge and dish storage are concealed in cabinetry. At the very end of the room by the windows rest chairs and tables to create a cozy reading area.

Facing Page: To maximize the space formerly used as a walk-in pantry, we built a wall of cabinetry. A Sub-Zero freezer occupies the far left, while glass doors in the center conceal walnut roll-out drawers for food storage use. The right-side cabinets also function as a pantry.
Photographs by Emily Minton Redfield

Above & Facing Page: At the hearth, the space goes slightly traditional. To the left and right of the range we laid CaesarStone countertops. A contemporary glass mosaic backsplash lends a dose of freshness and liveliness, while the frosted glass on the cabinet doors adds interest. The pot-filler faucet is a fun and functional touch.

Following Pages: We often continue our designs and innovations into the family room that usually adjoins the kitchen. In the living area opening off the kitchen right where the two islands converge, we brought in pops of blue to connect the rooms. A limestone hearth in a transitional style and polished nickel grids in the cabinet doors establish warmth.
Photographs by Emily Minton Redfield

"Don't sacrifice functionality for aesthetics. Let's develop the best working plan, then start adding the design elements." *Mikal Otten*

Garrity Design Group

Texas

Commitment, style, vision. These words describe the design philosophy of Andrea Garrity, principal of Garrity Design Group, which is based in Houston, Texas. Andrea lives and works by the golden rule; she treats each homeowner exactly as she wants to be treated. She also understands that a large part of designing homes requires establishing relationships and trust. Gearing each design plan to the unique personalities of the people who live within the house, Andrea and her team translate lifestyles into timeless environments that are loved for years after the project's completion. With a keen awareness of scale and a love of juxtaposed textures, Andrea creates soothing spaces for everyday life.

Left: Classic meets contemporary. The library conveys an inviting atmosphere suited for working, reading, and quiet conversation. The mahogany paneling, cabinets, and hand-scraped walnut floors were used throughout the room to create warmth. With their elegantly slender cross bracing, the display cabinets have an architectural look that engages the eye as lighting showcases the antique dynasty collection. The juxtaposition of textures throughout the room complements the feeling of the home.
Photograph by Baxter Imaging LLC

Above: Scale is so important in a large space. The massive butterfly painting by Hunt Slonem mirrors the size of the mahogany built-in. The chenille rug and Fendi sofas provide an inviting space for family to congregate and watch television.
Photograph by Baxter Imaging LLC

Facing Page Top Left: A glance into the dining room with the handpainted Shanghai silk walls and hand-scraped walnut floors reveals the custom made Macassar ebony dining table that seats 14. Underneath, the wool and silk scratched rug adds a bit of texture to the otherwise sleek space.
Photograph by Baxter Imaging LLC

Facing Page Top Right: Unusual accents such as the mirror-and-wall sconces combination above the console table add a personal design element, a touch of something you probably won't see in any other home.
Photograph by Janet Lenzen

Facing Page Bottom: The master bathroom features marble countertops, showers, and floor. The marble floor slabs are inlaid with mahogany to complement the paneled walls. From the wet/dry shower that is divided by a solid sheet of glass, the heavily wooded backyard is visible.
Photograph by Baxter Imaging LLC

Previous Pages: The game room functions as three separate areas which allow for multi-generational gatherings: a seating area for watching television, an alligator textured bar for entertaining, and an area for playing games. The connected media room is perfect for cuddling up to watch a movie. A touch of textures throughout adds a three dimensional feeling to the space.
Photograph by Baxter Imaging LLC

"Design must reflect the style of each individual homeowner so no two designs are alike."
Andrea Garrity

In-Site Design Group

Colorado

The designers at In-Site Design understand that the home is a sanctuary, offering a retreat from the hectic pace of modern life. Through the use of clean lines and the integration of classic pieces, In-Site's signature is translating the homeowners' vision into reality. Meticulous craftsmanship, artistic attention to detail, and a commitment to personalized interaction with homeowners are the standards by which In-Site approaches interior design. A design leader in the Rocky Mountain Region, Colleen Johnson creates timeless spaces while expressing a unique sensitivity to homeowners' lifestyles. In-Site Design Group cares deeply about the aging and physically challenged and is ready to create beautiful design to meet every homeowner's needs.

Left: We transformed the urban loft in downtown Denver from a highly detailed dark cherry interior to a light contemporary space. Distinctive lighting details throughout the loft were an essential part of the dramatic transformation into the high-tech contemporary look the owners desired.
Photograph by Terri Fotheringham

"Innovative lighting, unique architectural details, and harmonious color palettes create essential drama."
Colleen Johnson

Top: The custom William Ohs kitchen was framed at the ceiling and floor by exquisitely crafted wood details. The decorative beams were specifically constructed to house the major lighting elements, creating a more streamlined look. Open to the living and dining areas, it was critical for us to create a sophisticated cabinet package.

Middle: In the dining room, strong, clean lines of the dining table, credenza, and chandelier were custom designed to support and mirror the powerful architecture of the home.

Bottom: The gentleman's study is a masterful example of our teamwork with visionary architect Rich Lubischer. We took advantage of the fine craftsmanship of K.Z. Smith to enhance the feel of the space. It's a delight to the senses and provides an atmosphere of thoughtfulness and elegant comfort.

Facing Page: A perfect summation of the diverse architectural elements used throughout the home, the custom stairway presents a stunning Craftsman style. The added use of contemporary elements, such as glass and wire mesh, ensures its fresh, 21st-century feel.
Photographs by Terri Fotheringham

Above: As the jewel-like centerpiece of the narrow California beach house, the all-glass elevator makes its mark on the design. It represents engineering and precision at its height of expression. We were seriously challenged by the elevator, but it was well worth the effort.

Facing Page Top: Open spaces for entertaining were at a premium in the home, so the furnishings and design needed to serve a variety of functions.

Facing Page Bottom: The hearth room of the beach house was designed to accommodate an intimate group. Architect Robert Griffin designed the fossil stone fireplace wall in collaboration with Green River Stone. It is the perfect accompaniment to the homeowners' significant art collection.
Photographs by William Gullette

"Design that exudes a quiet energy produces a retreat that revitalizes."
Colleen Johnson

JF Design

Colorado

Jane Freking of JF Design carefully crafts interiors that reflect the lifestyles and visions of each individual homeowner. For more than two decades she's accepted upscale residential, commercial, and hospitality commissions, lending her personal touch to incredibly distinctive spaces. Jane loves to watch the project take shape over the course of the design process, and the final reveal of dreams made reality is always her favorite part. Colorado-based, she's also aware that a mountain home requires a separate approach from a California oceanfront property, and prepares her design method accordingly. After listening extensively to the owners' hopes and requirements, Jane takes especial joy in finding and presenting them with truly extraordinary objects, fabrics, and items that fit their needs and their one-of-a-kind space exactly.

Left: The home combines urban chic contemporary with gracious Old World traditional; Osborne & Little fabrics in black, white, and crisp color reappear throughout the home, giving it a modern edge and a very dramatic palette. In the master bedroom, I paired a traditional four-poster bed with a mirrored chest and mixed prints, florals, stripes, and tone-on-tone fabrics.
Photograph by Ron Ruscio Photography

"The designer's role is to bring beauty, order, and energy to every interior landscape." *Jane Freking*

Above: I prefer for the dining chairs to stand alone, not match the table. Oval-back chairs upholstered in black and white with serpentine seats and tapered legs represent a natural, graceful silhouette for modern design.

Facing Page Top: We took the black-and-white scheme and infused red accents to warm the informal family room. The comfortable red leather chairs give a casual nod to the silk plaid drapes.

Facing Page Bottom: In the adjacent formal living room and entry, the glass and accessories draw out the sea blue color from the dining room's John Lennon artwork. The entry's charcoal walls make a dramatic entrance and perfect backdrop for the Art Deco mirrors and Allan Knight acrylic bench. As the passage into the home, the foyer should make a memorable statement.
Photographs by Ron Ruscio Photography

J M Kelly Interiors

Arizona

Some of Jeanette Kelly's fondest childhood memories are of the hours spent decorating her dollhouse with the wallpaper, rugs, and curtains she would create from her craft supplies. Later, after pursuing less creative careers, Jeanette turned to the Maryland Institute College of Art in Baltimore to help realize the dream behind those dollhouse moments—to create beautiful, livable rooms through her own design firm, J M Kelly Interiors. As a strong believer in continuing education, Jeanette attends trade shows and seminars on a regular basis to ensure her designs embrace current trends while remaining classic and timeless. Drawing inspiration from her global travels, she engages in a collaborative process with homeowners. Jeanette specializes in space planning, color, and lighting, and supervises every step of the process from conception to completion, making the experience as easy as possible for the homeowners. Her designs are characterized by the layering of materials and light, creating richly dynamic spaces that not only work for the owners' lifestyles, but are also beautiful to behold.

Left: What began as a new sofa purchase became a full remodel of the living room. I found inspiration for the soaring fireplace from my experience sitting in the living room of Frank Lloyd Wright's Taliesin West. His use of boulders in a relatively small space created an unexpected balance and warmth. Emulating this, I created a façade for the fireplace that extends to the ceiling. The gas burner and crushed glass fill complete the transformation. I chose warm, textural furnishings for year-round comfort, and the seating is perfectly suited for the diminutive lady of the house.
Photograph by Geoffrey Hodgdon

Above Left: Handmade by a relative of the homeowner, bargello pieces were repurposed for the backs of the barstools. The kitchen was completely remodeled to provide more countertop workspace and to accommodate modern appliances, which are larger than those originally placed in the kitchen. I stepped the wall cabinets back to accommodate the microwave. The detail serves the dual purpose of giving the cabinet the proper depth to hold the appliance and providing architectural interest in the room.

Above Right: An oversized aqua Murano glass chandelier accentuates the vaulted ceiling in the master bedroom. The juxtaposition of the rough redwood ceiling and the smooth glass creates instant glamour in the space. The homeowner noticed the fixture while watching a television program and she was able to describe it in such a way that I could locate the seller. It gives the room an unparalleled wow factor.

Left: I faced the challenge of dealing with a small room that needed plenty of seating and storage space for a dining room. Open spaces in the cabinetry and the use of a glass-topped table keep the room inviting and light. Up to eight people can sit at the table, which is sculptural in its construction; it adds interest to the space without cluttering the limited square footage.

Facing Page: It's my belief that every home needs a quiet space where one or two people can read or have a conversation. The corner of a much larger living room made the perfect place for such an intimate seating arrangement. Neutral tones enhanced by varied textures make the space visually interesting, while the symmetrical arrangement of the chairs, table, and metal art panels provides simple elegance.
Photographs by Geoffrey Hodgdon

Above: Even in a large home, multipurpose spaces are very useful. The master bedroom was designed to have a generous area near the expanse of windows for watching television, reading, or chatting on the phone. Motorized blackout draperies were included in the design to make the room even more versatile, allowing for perfect movie watching in the height of the day. Chandeliers hung on either side of the bed are backed by six-foot metal-framed mirrors constructed from antiqued mirror panels.
Photograph by Scott Sandler

Facing Page Top: I created the illusion of a much larger space in the gentleman's office by playing with linear arrangements. Ceiling-height drapery panels, a diagonal flooring pattern, and built-in storage and countertop areas help to trick the eye into thinking the room is larger than reality. I used a clear glass desk in the center of the room to take up as little visual space as possible while providing an additional work surface.
Photograph by Scott Sandler

Facing Page Bottom: Starting with the existing furniture, which had to remain in the room, I used heavily embellished bedding and window treatments that combine three layers of textures to achieve a luxe look for the master bedroom. The custom upholstered headboard incorporates all three fabrics used throughout the design. Updated lamps reflect the calm sophistication that the homeowner desired; the result is a tightly coordinated and elegant look.
Photograph by Geoffrey Hodgdon

"Whether tactile or visual, texture enhances the richness of a design."
Jeanette Kelly

Above: A 12-foot island and a 10-foot bar anchor the space where the kitchen and the great room meet. The slate tile that lines the curved wall of the island and the flat surface of the backsplash reminded me of a rolltop desk. Hung vertically along the curve of the large island, the tile helps to keep the design cohesive throughout while adding a linear architectural element to a curved piece. Matching blown glass pendants with iron detailing were hung over both seating areas.

Facing Page Top: With views of the blue Arizona sky, the Black Mountains, and the Sonoran Desert, the living room is a place of comfort and serenity. I used locally common neutral colors as well as living and dried plants to visually merge the indoors and outdoors, extending the space beyond the home's walls. Furnishings and accessories effortlessly flow through the room and are centered around a simple round glass and Plexiglas coffee table. The shape of the room and the spectacular views were my inspiration; the shallow angle of the sectional mimics the angled window that is shaded by an automated solar screen installed at the perimeter of the patio overhang.

Facing Page Bottom Left: Unusual hanging pendants, an impressive recessed mirror, luxurious chocolate marble, and a carved-wood vanity combine to create the focal point of the powder room. Faux-finished walls richly layered with tones of purple, brown, and metallic bronze result in a rich tone that feels like the inside of a jewelry box, which was my inspiration.

Facing Page Bottom Right: Because the breakfast nook was such a special space, I chose interesting seating that wouldn't obscure the view. Elaborate drapery fixtures, such as the pegs used in the nook, draw your eye toward the sweeping scenery. The versatile furnishings can be used elsewhere in the home. Seating anywhere from two to 10 people, the dining table is perfect for flexible entertaining needs.
Photographs by Scott Sandler

Kristina Wolf Design

California

At the outset of her career, Kristina Wolf considered becoming an interior designer or a police officer. She ultimately chose to serve as a decorated public servant before her still-burning passion for design led her to enroll in design school at U.C. Berkeley. An impressed professor advised her to proceed straight to opening her own firm, so in 2007 she opened Kristina Wolf Design. She's been providing the Bay Area and Northern California with thoughtful, fresh design ever since. Skills gleaned from police work—the ability to read people, to truly listen, to find common ground amid conflict—are extremely useful, and by the end of the process even couples married for years tell her they learned something new about their spouse. Kristina always acts as her homeowners' advocate first, designing within the parameters requested but also enhancing the ideas with her own expertise as needed.

Left: Working within the five-story renovated San Francisco firehouse's beautiful, historic, and challenging architectural framework, we created a dramatic yet intimate living and dining space. The tall ceilings, apparatus bay doors, and original fire pole are elements we took into consideration when designing the ideal place for entertaining and relaxed living.
Photograph by David Duncan Livingston

"I seek a middle ground that incorporates a bit of everything, from the edgy to the safe. But I always try to encourage my homeowners to step outside their comfort zone just a little." *Kristina Wolf*

Above & Facing Page Top: In the firehouse living room, we floated a custom-made sectional of boiled wool fabric on top of a soft textured rug. Another custom-made piece, a coffee table inscribed with the periodic table of elements, grounds the conversation-friendly zone, and artwork and pillows add pops of color. The five "Heads of State" paintings in the dining area playfully join the other guests for dinner.

Facing Page Middle: The media room is where the homeowner unwinds and listens to music, and the design took cues from his love of travel and world culture. Masculine color tones and unique furnishings make it a bold room for entertaining as well. The nine ethnic masks on the wall framing the television add a tribal look and balance out the sleek modern furniture.

Facing Page Bottom: The views from the fifth-floor suite were a key factor in the master bedroom design. Using a minimalist approach, we highlighted the room's open and airy feeling by using light-colored bedding offset by a custom-made, wall-mounted headboard in dark wood and leather.
Photographs by David Duncan Livingston

Above: A busy world traveler's living room needed to highlight the architecture of the space and play to the owner's eclectic personality. I selected different textures, patterns, furnishings, and colors and arranged them to converge and harmonize into one soothing retreat.

Right: Large-scale chairs punctuate the adjacent dining room as the main statement pieces. Modern and global elements—representative of the owner's two worlds—blend into one artistic space pleasing to the eye.

Facing Page Top: A young executive and his family needed a sophisticated room for entertaining guests that could double as a durable, functional family room. Calling attention to the architectural elements—the fireplace, windows, nooks, and bookcases—honors the Craftsman style, and then I layered in some fun, modern flair on that base.

Facing Page Bottom: The Craftsman home's dining room and entryway both make an impact in the home. The dining room needed to be as fun yet sophisticated as the living room, and I enlarged the feel of the small room through color, shapes, and pieces that draw the eye in various directions. The artwork in the entry—the inspiration for the whole house design—acts as the focal point. The wall paint emphasizes the woodwork, while the bench seat and soft furnishings transform the space into an inviting, visually appealing room with seating.

Photographs by Chipper Hatter

Plush Home

California

Daughter of a renowned Italian sculptor, Nina Petronzio's artistic sensibilities and dedication to true craftsmanship serve her well in her pursuits as a master of interiors and furniture design. Founder of Los Angeles-based Plush Home, the full-service interior design firm and furniture manufacturer, Nina has an eye for elegant, classic-contemporary design. Her exquisitely appointed interior solutions, tailored to the individual lifestyle of the inhabitants of each space, have won her an elite list of clientele, including the Montage Hotel Beverly Hills and celebrities like Leonardo DiCaprio and Mark Wahlberg. Nina's furniture designs for Plush Home, hand-crafted in Los Angeles from premium-quality materials, are staple selections with Hollywood set designers, design mavens, and influential hotels. Nina accepts project worldwide, and specializes in turn-key custom homebuilding and remodels in the Los Angeles area.

Left: I streamlined the contemporary tri-level home on Mulholland Drive, bringing it more in line with its true form by replacing out-of-place features with handsome details designed to refocus attention on the home's glorious city and canyon views. I painted the dark finished doors and trims to shades of white, replaced all divided windows with single panes, redesigned the doors, and installed more proportional and refined mouldings. Many of these changes also gave the homeowner his preferred contemporary, masculine, and serene aesthetic. The master bedroom's sitting area reflects the subtle color scheme highlighted by bolder-hued throw pillows, accessories, and fine art.
Photograph by Laura Hull

Above, Right & Facing Page: The classic-contemporary home's formal living room, pool entry hallway, and dining room feature understated décor which complements the natural colors of the canyon visible through the many wide windows. Many of the entirely bespoke furnishings, made of varying wood from magohany to wenge to Macassar ebony, were first-generation additions to the Plush Home collection and have since become mainstays.

Photographs by Laura Hull

"My role is to express my homeowners' personal tastes and individuality through my eyes."
Nina Petronzio

Above & Facing Page: For the California Ranch home, I collaborated with our staff architect and builder to add a new downstairs wing that includes three children's room, two baths, a shared playroom, and an outdoor cabana and pool. I brought in the traditional feel, bold colors, and luxurious amenities my homeowners were accustomed to from their world travels. The sitting room, living room, and master bedroom exude upscale warmth and a casual, unpretentious family-oriented atmosphere. All furnishings were custom-made in Los Angeles from our collection, and most were accompanied by fine European fabrics.
Photographs by Laura Hull

Tucker & Marks

California

Grand estates, expansive gardens, and the timeless architecture of 1920s Santa Barbara delighted the eyes of interior designer Suzanne Tucker when she was a child. The exquisite environment is reflected in her tastes today: elegant and refined, classic, appropriate, and approachable. After earning a degree in design, Suzanne worked first in the fashion industry and then under San Francisco interior designer Michael Taylor, whom she credits with mentoring her design talents and sensibilities. In 1986, she and partner—now husband—Timothy Marks established their eponymous firm, Tucker & Marks. From those early days the firm has expanded to include different divisions: an in-house architecture department, furniture design, textiles, product development, and even tabletop lines. The firm is a virtual beehive of energy and activity where every idea is valued and considered—the ultimate think-tank of the service industry Tucker & Marks has taken by storm.

Left: In such a traditional space you might expect dressy curtains, but I wanted the room to feel open. I cidn't want to deemphasize the classical moulding in any way, so I installed simple, vanilla-colored matchstick blinds that filter light and give privacy without detracting from the room's architecture. A rare pair of 18th-century William Kent armchairs sit on either end of a 19th-century bamboo-topped Chinese daybed that serves as an oversized coffee table. Rock crystal pieces add organic sparkle to the space.
Photograph by Matthew Millman ·

"No matter what the style of a room is, it should feel current and 'of today.' No one wants to feel like they've stepped into a museum when in fact it's a home." *Suzanne Tucker*

Above: Antique doors lead into the naturally-lit breakfast area. Natural linen shades, tobacco-colored rattan chairs, and a walnut table bring the outdoors in. I always try to incorporate greenery into my designs—it gives the room a living, organic quality. The pop of green against the sand and wood tones brightens the eating area.

Facing Page: Pale straw, golden honey, and rich creams create a tranquil, natural feel to spaces that overlook beautiful sights beyond the home's four walls. Textured stone, sandblasted and hand-hewn woods, and a mixture of fabrics add a modern but cozy feel to the spaces.
Photographs by Matthew Millman

Amirob Interiors

Colorado—Arizona

Amirob Interiors principal Mickey Ackerman, Israeli-born, named his 1973-founded firm "Amirob," or "come to life" in Hebrew. The word applies to every project he and his team tackle: every design venture should make the homeowner feel like their dream home has come to life. The foremost goal of Mickey and his intimate team is to achieve their homeowners' most cherished wishes, and nothing less. Design revolves fully around the consumer at Amirob.

Left: The Boulder home rewrites the old adage about people in glass houses. While the views are fantastic, floors, ceiling, and walls of glass mean temperature control and privacy are challenges. The mountains and rock cropping surrounding the house inspired the design and décor.
Photograph by J. Curtis Photography

"Large-scale spaces require large-scale design and furnishings."
Mickey Ackerman

Above: The clever usage of glass furniture allowed us to tackle the challenge of designing the floating library–office. The hand-forged contemporary bases contrast well with the glass for an interesting look that captures perfectly the essence of a glass house.

Facing Page: To tie the kitchen and dining room together, we took an eight-ton rock and made it a water feature. The ceiling floats from the interior out for true indoor-outdoor living.
Photographs by J. Curtis Photography

"One thing we're known for is our powder rooms. Every guest will visit it, so it's become our hallmark to pay a lot of attention to that space." *Mickey Ackerman*

Above & Right: From the living room, sightlines extend 60 to 80 miles in the distance. Around the window-walls are glass floor insets, which we frosted for comfort. We kept the décor minimal and Zen so that it wouldn't clash with the views. In the master bath, we chose granite piece by piece to create a sky illusion: when inside the room, the granite appears part of the sky. It seamlessly integrates into the space.

Facing Page: From the exterior, the floating master bedroom could be a bird's nest supported by great posts that resemble cattails from the garden below. The great room, containing the living, dining, and kitchen areas, has been finished out with a restrained hand to allow natural beauty to shine. *Photographs by J. Curtis Photography*

Above: The professional-grade kitchen, open to the entire environment, needed to be fitted with elements that had the feel of fine furniture. To that end, we utilized three species of wood: striped mahogany, zebra, and lace. Then we selected the perfect granite to complement the water feature and rock slab. To create more storage, we dreamed up a series of floating cabinets with glass on the front and back to keep the panorama unhindered.

Right: In the master bedroom sitting room, three 12-foot glass walls look out to the Rockies and a meadow where 400 deer graze daily. We devised electric window shades for when the homeowners need privacy.

Facing Page: Glass ceilings magnify the theme of clarity throughout the property. The rock croppings within and without the walls of the house are really what inspired us; we love the connection to nature. A 3,000-gallon outdoor pond allows large koi fish to frolic.
Photographs by J. Curtis Photography

Barbatelli Signature Interiors

Colorado

Lovedy Barbatelli's notable linage, infused with her cultivated vision and classic ideals defines her signature style and inspires her career as an interior designer. Lovedy takes the tradition of design and combines it with her modern aesthetic, honing her vision and ability to interpret a person's lifestyle. The association and appreciation she possesses for fine art contributes to her intuitive expression. Lovedy's innate skill transforms lifestyle into a classical, timeless modernism that is sought after from coast to coast. She experiments with all the variables of form, function, and style, and reveals a composition of sophisticated elegance that embodies her clientele's character and style of living.

Left: I wanted to maintain a clean, minimal atmosphere without leaving the space feeling too austere. Softly textured grasscloth with splashes of color creates flair and interest. The cocktail table top is vintage 1970s terrazzo with a custom-designed base, and I also custom designed the wood mantle. An antique heirloom angel complements the art above the fireplace, which is a photograph taken by Kendrick Moholt of a Chris Antemann sculpture. The photograph serves as both a room anchor and an edgy focal point.
Photograph by Ron Ruscio and Jason Yung

Above: The rooftop patio invites the homeowner and guests to enjoy the outdoors with a bird's-eye view. A monochromatic palette keeps the space in harmony with the gray and white stucco exterior of the home. The expansive alfresco escape under an open sky offers all who visit a touch of luxury. Built-in planters and garden beds provide spaces to grow organic vegetables within the urban structure.

Facing Page Top: The master bedroom is inspired by Balinese design, featuring rich color and open architecture. The large bed wall is covered in striking, flocked wallpaper, which adds alluring appeal. Extra storage is integrated into the design with an entire wall of ample closet space.

Facing Page Bottom Left: Authentic silver-leaf and a vintage Italian "Dandelion" light fixture from the 1900s make the office a true showstopper. I designed the desk myself, and it's a great workstation as well as an eye-catching addition to the room.

Facing Page Bottom Right: The "Den of Lips," a powder room, features sophisticated yet funky wallpaper from France and a cork-tiled backsplash. The bright shade of green is the perfect complement to the living room.
Photographs by Ron Ruscio and Jason Yung

"Details determine destiny." *Lovedy Barbatelli*

Brandenburg Studios

Oregon

The husband and wife team behind Brandenburg Studios represents a marriage of design and craftsmanship. With founder Betsy Brandenburg Hurst's nearly two decades of experience in interior design and remodeling, and her husband Brian Hurst's background as an artist and craftsman, a harmonious and well-rounded design team is formed. Whether the home is vintage or contemporary, Brandenburg Studios focuses on collaborating with its homeowners to create a sense of timelessness inspired by the local vernacular and spectacular landscapes of the Pacific Northwest.

Left: The original plan for the home's entry belied its prime location by the Columbia River. Separated from the living area and its view by a long dark hallway, the entry was unwelcoming. We opened up the plan so you get an immediate view of the river upon entering the home. Moving toward the light, you find yourself in a gallery space, which encourages you to linger as ever-expanding views unfold. The gallery was inspired by the homeowner's love of Northwestern art, much of which was commissioned specifically for the space.
Photograph by Andrea Johnson Photography

Above: The simple form of the home's cabinetry is animated by the intricate figuring in the anigre wood. It catches the light and dances on sunny days, and its golden tone brings the space warmth on the many grey days we enjoy here in the Pacific Northwest. The dining room furnishings were designed to blend seamlessly with the watery tones outside.

Left: The painting above the bed reminded me of the view looking up toward the surface while swimming underwater. This was perfect, not only for the riverside location of the home but because the homeowner also loves to scuba dive. These deep, watery blues inspired the layered palette of the custom bedding. Silk accents in the area rug sparkle in the light like reflections on the surface of water.

Facing Page Bottom: Throughout the home, clean contemporary lines are softened and enlivened by visual or tactile textures. The clean, arcing form of the fireplace contrasts with the rough limestone surround and custom-cast glass pulls. Almost everything in the home was commissioned or custom designed by local artists and craftsmen. I designed the one-of-a-kind sofa and cocktail tables specifically for the room. Inspiration struck during a walk on the beach outside when Brian and I noticed the lovely pattern the river creates in the wet sand. I had the craftsmen re-create this pattern in carving the tables. The light plays off the surface, mimicking the view outside.

Photographs by Andrea Johnson Photography

Genchi Interior Design

California

As an architecture student who was captivated by the "prettier things," Leslie Genchi switched over to the realm of interior design and discovered her lifelong passion. Echoing her sudden shift in career choice, the founder of Genchi Interior Design continues to brazenly forge her own standards for what is beautiful and works well by creating her own color schemes, breaking traditional rules of interior design, and ultimately doing what she wants. Leslie takes risks in her projects with contemporary and unconventional qualities that ask homeowners to take daring steps outside of their comfort zone. In doing so, she continually grows as a designer unbounded.

Left: The homeowners had a living room that was disconnected from the kitchen space. Using a contemporary color scheme that juxtaposed warm and cool tones, I created a nontraditional space marked by black and white contrast with strong red accents, bridging the two separate rooms. Bold curtain patterns, which are also replete in the kitchen, give the room some additional pop.
Photograph courtesy of Genchi Interior Design

"Rules are boring."
Leslie Genchi

Above: The contrast between the dark wood flooring and cabinetry alongside bold white chairs and the cow-print rug creates interest and draws the eyes around the vibrant room. I used two translucent Lucite chairs to give the perception of more space in a contemporary kitchen area.

Facing Page: Originally built at floor level, I raised the existing fireplace a few feet to a visually stunning height that grounds the room with its contrast against the white wall.
Photographs courtesy of Genchi Interior Design

"Each room has its own personality and it's all about tying every room together." *Leslie Genchi*

Left: A door leading to the kitchen made the room a confusing area that was too crowded for the homeowners. The custom turquoise banquette offers seating at little expense to the spatial flow of the room. Working with the original wall color instead of painting over it, I added stripe-patterned curtains and a glass chandelier over the table, making the room more compelling.
Photograph courtesy of Genchi Interior Design

"It's a myth that strong colors make a room look smaller." *Leslie Genchi*

Above: I like to emphasize the walls and floors while keeping major pieces like sofas in neutral beige colors, tying every room together with a timeless, versatile look. The striped curtains—which reoccur throughout the interior—and the tiger-skin rug do a good job of making their spaces exciting. Instead of painting all the walls in the dark teal color, I highlighted the room by painting the ceiling a creamy white.

Facing Page: In the office, the walls feature a retro-modern pattern that unites the dark teal color of one room to the beige and orange hues of another room. Sparking an interaction between warm and cool tones, I introduced elements of brown, seen in the floor and desk, to the silvery qualities of the chairs, chandelier, and lamp.
Photographs courtesy of Genchi Interior Design

Above: The coved ceiling was an interesting challenge because it provided no corners to work with and the homeowners wanted the walls painted blue without painting the ceiling. Using the moulding around the room to demarcate the walls from the ceiling, we painted the walls in a light turquoise, leaving the ceiling white to accentuate the colors.

Left: Accents such as a chandelier and a coral-inspired fruit bowl bring an element of liveliness to the interior while also bridging different rooms together with their common theme of playfulness.

Facing Page: Inspired by warm Tuscan and Southwestern colors, the brown curtains, yellow walls, and red rug blend together comfortably. Seeing how a typical sofa would take up too much space in a room that needed flow, I used a custom sofa sectional in a buttery yellow color suitable to the color scheme.
Photographs courtesy of Genchi Interior Design

JJ Interiors

Colorado

Sleek and chic is the mantra for the contemporary designs by Jennifer Jelinek, ASID, of JJ Interiors. Many of her designs are based on sleek lines and clean textures with simplified colors and pared-down details, which she believes is all extremely important to successfully achieving a modern style. Jennifer doesn't skimp on the details, though. They become even more vital in a contemporary setting, as they are completely exposed and fewer in number. Working in tandem with homeowners' expectations, Jennifer creates a cohesive feel throughout every project, like repeating elements in several rooms in a home to provide continuity. She warms otherwise cold and sterile environments with natural elements like stone, wood, and metal to provide a strong, clean backdrop that ultimately brings each room's look together seamlessly.

Left: Keeping the living space comfortable and open to the kitchen provides a great entertainment space, allowing the homeowners to never be separated from the gathering area. For more casual affairs, we included a pop-up television inside the custom-designed wood cabinet next to the fireplace. We really wanted to allow those great expansive views of the foothills to be one of the most dynamic art pieces in the house, so we focused on the large windows and framing the views.
Photograph by Ron Ruscio

Above: When guests walk through the front door, their eye is carried through that main entry to the outdoors. So we really used the exterior setting to help inspire the color palette as well as some of the design elements within the house.

Facing Page: A powder room is definitely one area homeowners want to pay special attention. It's a space that all the guests use; it's the day-to-day bathroom in a house, so we don't want to neglect it. By doing floor-to-ceiling tile on the wall—a contemporary mosaic out of natural materials—combined with clean vertical lines of the mirror, a sleek faucet, and streamlined concrete countertop, the blend of natural elements impart balance for this space.

Photographs by Ron Ruscio

"My role is to design for my homeowners, so the end results reflect their personal tastes and the space truly feels like their home. What they need, how they live, and design with great function and style are all of the utmost importance."
Jennifer A. Jelinek

"Textural elements become very important when you're using a monochromatic palette. They provide interest in an otherwise simple design." *Jennifer A. Jelinek*

Above: The kitchen needed to be eminently functional, act as a warm gathering place, and also fit the modern aesthetic of the home. The lyptus slab cabinet doors with vertical graining integrate green materials into the design while introducing clean lines. To break up the large, single-height island and define the seating area, we inset a round CaesarStone cutout within the larger L-shaped granite countertop. Combining natural stone with metal in the backsplash highlights the balance of earthy and contemporary.

Facing Page Top: Bathrooms are becoming increasingly important in the design of a house. They're a space that homeowners are spending more and more time relaxing in, especially with elements like steam showers and Jacuzzi tubs. The requirements for space, comfort, and storage are increasingly more important, as well as providing separate his and hers areas. Taking advantage of the space we had available in this master bathroom, we were able to create a central vanity that looks like it's floating. The sinks are back-to-back with a suspended mirror in between them, offering a clean, open, and airy ambience.

Facing Page Bottom: The wine room with sliding glass doors that are on an industrial-looking track provides visibility and integration into the space but allows it to become a separate room. The concept of the neighborhood was a European hillside. We took it a fresh, contemporary direction as if an old Tuscan home were renovated and modernized. Some rooms lean more contemporary and some have more elements reminiscent of Old World style, like in the wine room, while still maintaining great continuity and flow throughout the home.
Photographs by Ron Ruscio

Kalleen & Company

Indiana

Chip Kalleen's statement to his clientele is straight-forward and direct, reflecting his no-nonsense approach to design. His interest in design was sparked at an early age and he attributes this, in large part, to the childhood home that his parents built in Lexington, Kentucky. Today, that house is a fine example of mid-century modern, but back in the late 1950s, it was simply a contemporary home with vaulted ceilings, large angular windows, and ribbed fiberglass wall panels. It was not until Chip was older that he realized just how much that home influenced his passion for design. Now his environments provide an immediate sense of scale and proportion. He chooses materials, finishes, colors, lighting, layout, furnishings, and art that truly define, enhance, elevate, and celebrate the individual. In essence, each of his completed projects is a perfect reflection of the homeowner's personality and lifestyle.

Left: The Indianapolis urban condo, which I initially designed while at Lohr Design, Inc., required a design concept to complement, not detract from, the expansive floor-to-ceiling treetop views of the parks and memorials below. The windows act as art, framing views of an ever-changing panorama from morning to night. Interior architectural details were downplayed with the exception of the custom, ruby red blown glass chandelier highlighting the home's two-story atrium. Furnishings have been kept purposely low and their overall lines clean and simple. Richly textured and generally neutral-toned fabrics were selected and accented with earthy reds and oranges, creating an interior that is as bright and vibrant as it is warm and inviting.
Photograph by Megan Van Valer of MV2 Photography, inc.

Above: In the new entertainment area, the music and conversation space on the west side of a raised platform is dominated by a large angled banquette that provides generous space for guests to gather in comfort. The banquette's recessed base features soft lighting that visually floats the unit and lightens its overall impact in the space. Even with the home's grand panoramic views to the north, west, and south, the room remains intimate and cozy through its modulated ceiling heights and low-set banquette and leather ottomans. A black lacquer piano, sitting in a windowed bay, boldly reflects activity from within and outside the space while contemporary glass elements add dramatic bursts of color.

Facing Page Top Left: In designing the condo's recent expansion, I remodeled the original entryway to create a more luxurious and spacious passage separating the home's more quiet, private areas from the active entertainment spaces. A pale marble mosaic floor and the coral-hued Venetian plaster wall are the perfect backdrops for the eight-foot bow-front console table in black lacquer.

Facing Page Top Right: The intimate circular sitting area on the north side of the atrium features a custom rug from Edward Fields and matching seating in the living room. Low-rise lacquered display cabinets define the raised platform area and provide a deep countertop and lit niches to display a growing art collection.

Facing Page Bottom Left: Backlit, cast-glass stair treads lead to the raised platform area. A massive ledgestone slate wall with a see-through fireplace separates the music and conversation area from the movie lounge.

Facing Page Bottom Right: Cabinetry in curly maple provides display space for the contemporary glass collection as well as storage for entertaining needs.
Photographs by Megan Van Valer of MV2 Photography, Inc.

"My work is about texture and contrast, scale and proportion, and design simplicity. I like crisp lines, minimal detailing, and mixing the lowly with the sublime for an overall look that is fresh and cleanly edited." *Chip Kalleen*

Left: The Carmel, Indiana, residence backs up to a deep woods but looked at odds with this natural setting due to its distracting multicolored brick façade. Painting all the brick an earthy neutral moss color enabled the home to blend into its surroundings. A Zen garden at the front leads quietly to a raised deck where backlit risers glow softly at night. The entrance, virtually transparent, features a dramatically lit bronze sculpture.

Below: The living room was transformed by eliminating the sunken floor and the fireplace's traditional raised hearth. Sheathing the fireplace in cold rolled steel added texture, scale, and drama, as did selecting dark natural slate tiles for the flooring. Sleek painted cabinetry with lit display niches showcase the art collection. Furnishings include mid-century classics and warm, richly grained Scandinavian wood pieces.

Facing Page Top: Black granite wraps the island in the contemporary kitchen, pairing beautifully with the white glass backsplash and slate floors. The warmth and dramatic graining of the anigre wood cabinets provide just the right amount of crispness and contrast. Classic Saarinen chairs add a burst of saturated color in the nearby dining area.

Facing Page Left: The sunroom's three walls of glass blur the line between inside and out and supply a connection to the flora and fauna beyond. A richly hued cowhide rug provides strong texture and vibrant natural pattern while anchoring a seating group consisting of Eames Lounge chairs, a Noguchi cocktail table, and a striking Italian loveseat.

Facing Page Right: The bright and airy master bath was created in the original master bedroom's footprint. A wall of sculpted glass blocks provides abundant light and softly distorts views for privacy. The slate floor anchors the free-standing sculpted tub and slopes gently to the water wall for the ultimate shower experience. Clear glass panels separate the wet area from the sink area and its long cantilevered vanity of rich mahogany. *Photographs by Megan Van Valer of MV2 Photography, Inc.*

Orlando Diaz-Azcuy
Design Associates

California

Thanks to a background in architecture, Orlando Diaz-Azcuy approaches his interior design projects with discipline and focus. A pragmatic problem solver, he avoids all pretention when putting together a new project, making sure every object he incorporates into a space has purpose. Orlando delves into each individual component of a design, laying out rooms that are a meaningful reflection of the homeowner. His appreciation of understated elements produces pristine environments devoid of frills and flamboyancy, and each room exhibits a subtle, flawless elegance. With tireless attention to detail, Orlando creates spaces with a clear vision from conception to completion.

Left: David T. Oldroyd, a principal at ODADA, Orlando Diaz-Azcuy Design Associates, loves going home every day. One look around his living quarters, and it's easy to see why. He gave his early 20th-century Edwardian a stellar upgrade with a clean, crisp palette. Its soft shades of green, grey, and beige soften the more rigorous lines of the home's new interior architecture, while varied textures give the space interest and depth. A cypress tree trunk dining table offers a casual place to relax, while the nearby 19th-century chaises with diamond tufting create a dialogue with the spectacular art piece behind it. The piece by Andrew Kudless, entitled *P-Wall*, is made of cast plaster.
Photograph by Nathan Kirkman

"Never compromise on quality. Plan, wait, save, and pursue what you really want. One object of great quality is worth a dozen of mediocrity."
David T. Oldroyd

Above: Sitting beneath a reflection of David's piano, which he plays as a concert pianist, is a lacquered 13-foot modern credenza designed by David. It contrasts the walls, covered in a paint that appears white in the sun's bright light but transforms into a pale green as night approaches.

Facing Page Top Left: Offering quietude after a day's work, the master bedroom's wraparound deck—enclosed with boxwood hedging instead of railing—overlooks the city's panorama. A seamless transition between inside and out exists in the space, and small succulents displayed on the contemporary seating area play into the theme.

Facing Page Top Right: An eight-foot looped wire mesh sculpture by Ruth Asawa hangs at the top of the stairwell, leading up to the master bedroom.

Facing Page Bottom Left: David enjoys designing things in pairs, and demonstrates this affection in the living room with two 19th-century English chaises. The oil-on-canvas painting above the mantle, discovered in a thrift store, is a striking contrast to the Hermes throw and Frank Gehry Wiggle chair.

Facing Page Bottom Right: A pair of 1970s fiberglass chairs sit near the kitchen, a space for guests to gather around the 1950s bronze and glass bar cart. A pair of black bi-fold panels hang behind the seating area, allowing the option to divide or close off designated spaces of the home.
Photographs by Nathan Kirkman

Above: Walls of hand-applied goldleaf invite a little glitter from the city into the interior. The home's simple yet elegant design theme is apparent throughout every corner of the space, as demonstrated by a 20th-century Josef Hoffman mirror, one of three in the apartment.

Facing Page: The sophisticated use of color in 12 contemporary oil panel paintings by Antonio del Moral gives the refined city apartment a bit of character. Rattan McGuire chairs designed by Orlando in an ebony finish with black fabric upholstery complement the white lacquer dining table. A side table with an iron base and limestone top furnish the dining area. *Photographs by Nathan Kirkman*

"A room is not complete until it's accessorized. Be sure to add the little things that bring you pleasure."
Orlando Diaz-Azcuy

Above: Floor-to-ceiling windows present a view of the bay and invite a deluge of sunlight into the space. Orlando's New York sofa from McGuire Furniture is upholstered in a basket weave cotton and linen fabric. Two late 1930s Art Deco chairs provide plenty of seating for guests. A side table with its custom Halila limestone top is perched between a pair of Copenhagen lounge chairs, also designed by Orlando for McGuire.

Facing Page Top: A custom area rug from Stark in silk and aloe grounds the space and provides a stage for the Paul Evans coffee table's sculptural metal base. Pillows made from antique Fortuny fabrics rest on the couch, creating a visual tie to the wall's gold leaf.

Facing Page Bottom Left: The master bath's entry is serene, featuring frosted glass closet doors.

Facing Page Bottom Right: A sliding panel door opens to reveal an office.
Photographs by Nathan Kirkman

"Strive for the best craftsmanship you can afford with the budget that you have."
Orlando Diaz-Azcuy

Above Left: With Japanese, Italian, and French influences, the living area suggests a worldly ambience. Welcoming visitors as they arrive, the entry features blue lacquered walls and a 1950s demi-lune Piero Fornasetti cabinet. English silver-plate candle holders rest on top, and an 18th-century Spanish giltwood and blue glass mirror hangs above.

Above Right: To suit the homeowners' fancy for entertaining, the design provides plenty of space to host a gathering. The home's eclectic pieces act as not only aesthetic elements but also as conversation starters among mingling partygoers. A Fornasetti folding screen graces the back wall.

Facing Page: A late 19th-century plaster relief of Victory hangs against white lacquer walls. Overhead, the Sputnik chandelier shines down upon a centerpiece filled with porcelain apples. Down the hall, a metal tree sculpture by Ruth Asawa sprouts from the countertop.
Photographs by Nathan Kirkman

"The most important element in the house is the homeowner. His or her personality must be clearly expressed in the space."
Orlando Diaz-Azcuy

Above: Customized Francois lounge chars and a sofa from Marco Fine Furniture upholstered in beeswax-toned chenille surround a coffee table with a cream parchment top. Two lamps with iron bases complement a hand-woven jute area rug. On the wall, four Italian tempera painted-paper panels hang in gilded frames, along with a Caio Fonseca print in a white lacquer frame. Down-filled pillows add a luxurious touch to the sofa.

Right: The homeowner enjoys wearing bright colors and rich patterns, so incorporating a bold hue into the space was essential. In the guest room, Chinese red-lacquered tea tables are a gorgeous accompaniment to the rust-colored Fortuny wall covering. A pair of Art Deco giltwood candlesticks provide another touch of warmth to the sitting area.

Facing Page: Carrara marble covers the floor, vanity top, and bath in the spa-like retreat. Polished nickel Art Deco sconces with pink silk shades flank the entryway. Through the doorway sits the dressing area draped in blood orange silk taffeta. A white mink throw lays upon the chaise, and a collection of evening gowns occupies the glamorous mirrored pear wood closet.
Photographs by Nathan Kirkman

index

index

Publishing Team

PUBLISHER: Brian G. Carabet

PUBLISHER: John A. Shand

ART DIRECTOR: Emily A. Kattan

GRAPHIC DESIGNER: London Nielsen

GRAPHIC DESIGNER: Lillian Oliveira

MANAGING EDITOR: Lindsey Wilson

EDITOR: Megan Winkler

MANAGING PRODUCTION COORDINATOR: Kristy Randall

DIRECTOR OF BOOK DEVELOPMENT : Rosalie Z. Wilson

ADMINISTRATIVE COORDINATOR: Amanda Mathers

Lilly Levy Designs, page 87

THE PANACHE COLLECTION

Dream Homes Series

An Exclusive Showcase of the Finest Architects, Designers and Builders

Carolinas, Chicago, Coastal California, Colorado, Deserts, Florida, Georgia, Los Angeles, Metro New York, Michigan, Minnesota, New England, New Jersey, Northern California, Ohio & Pennsylvania, Pacific Northwest, Philadelphia, South Florida, Southwest, Tennessee, Texas, Washington, D.C., Extraordinary Homes California

Spectacular Homes Series

An Exclusive Showcase of the Finest Interior Designers

California, Carolinas, Chicago, Colorado, Florida, Georgia, Heartland, London, Michigan, Minnesota, New England, Metro New York, Ohio & Pennsylvania, Pacific Northwest, Philadelphia, South Florida, Southwest, Tennessee, Texas, Toronto, Washington, D.C., Western Canada

Perspectives on Design Series

Design Philosophies Expressed by Leading Professionals

California, Carolinas, Chicago, Colorado, Florida, Georgia, Great Lakes, London, Minnesota, New England, New York, Pacific Northwest, South Florida, Southwest, Toronto, Western Canada

Art of Celebration Series

Inspiration and Ideas from Top Event Professionals

Chicago & the Greater Midwest, Colorado, Georgia, New England, New York, Northern California, South Florida, Southern California, Southern Style, Southwest, Toronto, Washington, D.C.

City by Design Series

An Architectural Perspective

Atlanta, Charlotte, Chicago, Dallas, Denver, New York, Orlando, Phoenix, San Francisco, Texas

Spectacular Wineries Series

A Captivating Tour of Established, Estate and Boutique Wineries

California's Central Coast, Napa Valley, New York, Ontario, Oregon, Sonoma County, Texas, Washington

Experience Series

The Most Interesting Attractions, Hotels, Restaurants, and Shops

Austin & the Hill Country, British Columbia, Thompson Okanagan

Interiors Series

Leading Designers Reveal Their Most Brilliant Spaces

Florida, Midwest, New York, Southeast, Washington, D.C.

Golf Series

The Most Scenic and Challenging Golf Holes

Arizona, Colorado, Ontario, Pacific Northwest, Southeast, Texas, Western Canada

Weddings Series

Captivating Destinations and Exceptional Resources Introduced by the Finest Event Planners

Southern California

Luxury Homes Series

High Style From the Finest Architects and Builders

Carolinas, Chicago, Florida

Specialty Titles

Publications about Architecture, Interior Design, Wine, and Hospitality

21st Century Homes, Distinguished Inns of North America, Into the Earth: A Wine Cave Renaissance, Luxurious Interiors, Napa Valley Iconic Wineries, Shades of Green Tennessee, Spectacular Hotels, Spectacular Restaurants of Texas, Visions of Design

Custom Titles

Publications by Renowned Experts and Celebrated Institutions

Cloth and Culture: Couture Creations of Ruth E. Funk, Colonial: The Tournament, Dolls Etcetera, Geoffrey Bradfield Ex Arte, Lake Highland Preparatory School: Celebrating 40 Years, Family Is All That Matters

Panache Books App

Inspiration at Your Fingertips

Download the Panache Books app in the iTunes Store to access select Panache Partners publications. Each book offers inspiration at your fingertips.

Panache Partners, LLC   Dallas, Texas   469.246.6060   www.panache.com